To Marion
In our Diamond Year

GILDED WALLS

A Guide to Climbers, Wall Shrubs and Fruit

Arranged according to the season of principal effect,
some spanning more than one season, particularly
evergreens and notably hedera and euonymus.

JIM PEARCE

First published 2005
Copyright © 2005 by James Pearce

ISBN 0-9550090-0-6

Published by James Pearce, Copford UK

Printed by Polestar Wheatons Ltd Exeter Devon EX2 8RP

Introducing the author

Jim Pearce was born in Birmingham in 1924 and later, due to parental insistence, a trade being the norm for young school-leavers in those days, he served an apprenticeship as an engineering pattern maker.

Following the end of the Second World War, he chose to reject industry and joined the staff at the College of the Ascension, Selly Oak, Birmingham as a gardener. He was eventually promoted to Head Gardener and began his writing career by contributing a weekly column to the *Birmingham Sunday Mercury* and as a regular contributor to *Garden News*.

At the end of the 1950s he joined the Daffodil Society and in 1959 became its secretary, which also meant being its Show Secretary and Editor of Publications as well, a postion he held for the next 25 years.

With the sale of the land at the College, Jim could not countenance the marginalisation of the garden he had striven to develop and maintain, and so he sought pastures new and became Head Gardener at Braxted Park in Essex.

A different fate awaited him there. After overhauling and improving the estate for some years, the lady of the house, who had taken a great interest in all he had done, died in tragic circumstances. Accordingly Jim moved on to work for Notcutts Nurseries as their Plantsman and took the opportunity to found his own daffodil nursery, Copford Bulbs, which proved very successful.

His gardening column also transferred to Colchester's local paper, *Essex County Standard*, which he still contributes today, and at that time he also became President of the Daffodil Society, a post he held for ten years.

On retiring from Notcutts he set up his own Landscaping Consultancy which has kept him extremely busy in both Essex and Suffolk, even to planning and planting a new arboretum.

Surprisingly he has also found time to serve on the Royal Horticultural Society's Daffodil and Tulip Committee for over 25 years as well as editing the annual *Daffodil and Tulip Yearbook* for some ten of them.

He was for more than 30 years a lecturer in Further Education in both Birmingham and Essex, was a founder member of the Professional Gardeners Guild, and still found time to adjudicate as a fellow of the National Vegetable Society nationwide.

With the welter of books on horticultural topics seemingly endless, to find a niche would seem well nigh impossible, but with his new book on climbing plants, wall shrubs and fruit I believe Jim has achieved this aim. His background of some 60 years' gardening experience, coupled with an easily readable style featuring numerous excellent plant portraits, presents us with a superb guide for both beginner and seasoned gardener alike.

Reg Nicholl

Acknowledgements

My appreciation is due to James and Wendy Akers without whose computer and other skills this publication would not have been possible and to Reg Nicholl for his detailed assistance.

Further credits to Garden Matters for images of *Ampelopsis* and *Aristolochia* on pages 106,107, Wendy Wesley from the Royal Horticultural Society, Wisley for *Vestia* on page 95, Sue Tasker for *Telopea* on page 93, The Magnolias Garden, Essex for *Colquhounia* on page 123, and Richard Smales for *Vine Weevils* on page 26.

The remaining pictures are my own.

Jim Pearce

Contents

Cover pictures

Front	*Sophora tetraptera*
Back upper left	*Clematis* 'Comtesse de Bouchard'
Back upper right	*Fremontodendron*
Back lower left	*Indigofera amblyantha*
Back lower right	Pear 'Doyenne de Comice'

Introduction

To many less fortunately placed gardeners the idyllic hope is that one day their ship will come in or the lottery turn up trumps, so they may have a place in the country to engage their whiles.

Whether or not their castles in the air become a reality will determine their future prospects, perhaps something on the grand scale or just making the most of whatever has become their lot. Possibly a semi in suburbia, a more modest terraced house or just a flat without even a garden of note. All will surely have walls that crave attention and perhaps fences demanding decoration to play a part in some more grandiose scheme.

Such thoughts conjure up ivy-covered walls and rose-bowered porches with lilies and hollyhocks growing with the abandon of those on a chocolate box cover. All in close proximity to the open lounge window that the perfumed air may add further charms to the seemingly endless quest to enjoy life to the full.

To adorn the cottage walls or hide the sharp features basic to any building is a natural inclination of gardeners, born with a desire to embellish and titivate every object that is not in itself productive of luxuriant growth or blossom. That damage to the very structures that the plants add lustre to, is a point avidly held by some, yet disputed with equal fervour by a far larger body as any trip around an estate will verify. Indeed the very profusion of leafage systematically angled to the heaven's most radiant star in themselves act as a foil to the falling rain and to a degree must be a further asset in the current clamour to double glaze and insulate. A few additional spiders perhaps but little or no chance of any natural plant predators taking up residence in the happy home.

The excessive droughts of 1975 and particularly 1976 disturbed the serenity of the cobwebbed offices of the property insurers seeking out the small print in an effort to lay all the blame at the feet of the enthusiastic planter for the sundry shiftings and cracking that befell a number of properties, especially those on heavy clay soils. I have witnessed instances where truly fine flourishing plants were unceremoniously ejected for their sins along with other cases where eagle-eyed underwriters had decreed the ultimate branch spread and not a leaf joint further. Local authority departments, always ready to slip on another shackle (not that I am in favour of total laissez-faire) lost no time in curtailing the eagerness of would-be planters of substantial growing shrubs or trees, scarcely within sight of any building. The underlying problem is that no serious work has been carried out on what is an extremely difficult subject to quantify. Architects and their hirelings are unlikely to have the hands-on experience of a professional gardener who has spent many years face to face not only with shoots and flowers, but equally with roots and all that these entail.

Roots are to water what shoots are to the sun, always seeking a source of the very life-giving nutrients dissolved in the residual moisture. These are much more likely to be found away from the absorbent brickwork than beneath the foundations, excepting some unusual circumstance requiring the intuition of a builder rather than that of a gardener.

Walls, and to a lesser degree fences, are a means to an end, giving one the opportunity to grow a far wider range of subjects than could otherwise be entertained. Their very presence providing shelter and a selection of micro-climatic conditions akin to their native heaths. So providing a home from home environment, to plants collected the world over to do duty in a range of conditions otherwise out of the question.

1
Aspect

Choosing the best aspect is of vital importance when selecting a home for one's plants. To subject a shade-loving shrub such as a camellia to an arid spot when it may well receive near microwave treatment is unlikely to give the desired result of a healthy, luxuriant and well-flowered subject. On the other hand to set a wisteria on a dull north-facing wall will have little chance of making a useful contribution to the general picture. Overall a west-facing fence or wall may be regarded as the truly safe bet. Provided it is not overhung by trees it will receive half a day's sun, escape the dehydrating easterly winter winds and likewise in spring frost damage to tender growths, such as those of the actinidia. It should not prove overburdening to the shade lovers though not entirely desirable. Its opposite counterpart, one facing due east will usually prove quite satisfactory for those of a deciduous character. Few evergreens will tolerate the easterlies especially in the earlier months. Surprisingly perhaps, campsis and wisterias are quite content, as are a clutch of slightly tender shrubs that have withdrawn their leafage from the winter scene. With the possibility of sun from dawn to dusk, at first thought the obvious hottest spot must be that offered by a south-facing wall. I recall the wisdom of a learned radio panellist of yesteryear, namely Professor Joad who became renowned for his epithet "it all depends", and so it does. If the eastern blow is blocked by a return of the building or fence, or suitably sheltered by some dense evergreen such as a holly or yew then the coveted gem will enjoy the full benefit that accrues from such a cosseted spot. By the same token north-facing positions are particularly suited to a number of natural woodland plants such as camellias but will suffer at flowering time if cold winds and more particularly frost are allowed full sway. Similar protection afforded that on the opposite point of the compass should ensure a safe passage.

Inevitably in compiling a miscellany of suitable plants for walls and fences the variation of form will vary dramatically. Some will be natural climbers while many others will simply be after the cosier conditions that such protection provides. Away from protective screening their life would perhaps be miserable at best while in many cases they would just be non-starters. In general, endemic plants from the western seaboard of America are not best pleased with the colder winters of this small island. Yet given a haven reminiscent of their native heath and a little tender loving care, they will perform as well as our own natives. True climbers do so by a variety of methods. Some, in no lesser manner than winding their stems, either clockwise or anti-clockwise, depending upon species, either into a nearby host to enjoy the attentions of the sun, or, perforce have little option than to ramble over the ground, perhaps at some point bedecking to good effect a forlorn obstacle. Others with less inclination to mimic a python are content to merely flex their leaf stalks, as the clematis does using them to clasp anything suitable in the support line on hand. Yet another rung on the would-be climber's ladder is the use made of suction pads formed at the extremity of tendrils so familiar on the Boston Ivy. The true ivy and climbing hydrangea develop aerial roots along their newly forming stems by fervently clinging to tree or wall.

Of the other group invariably collected in the "Climbing" section of nurserymen's catalogues, there are the less sophisticated scandent shrubs that are content to make their way in the world simply by prostrating one branch upon another so forming a tangled hummock as in the manner of our native bramble, until the mission of presenting their flowers to the sun is accomplished. Many such a spineless shrub is the stock in trade of the enthusiast who will save it from its misdemeanours, bring it back to the straight and narrow and in so doing transform an otherwise mundane subject into a star attraction.

Then there is that curious phenomenon, the herringbone cotoneaster, *C. horizontalis*. Shunning the attentions of the would-be trainer with shoulders to the wall or fence, it does little more than simply lean with amazing rigidity even in the face of gusting winds. Few share this DIY trait.

Many less hardy bulbous subjects, annuals and herbaceous plants benefit from the shelter of these climbing shrubs whereas in the open border they would present a poor rendition of their full potential, if even succeeding at all.

Besides the walls or fences proper, many a garden boasts a dry wall, invariably styled on the skilfully built features that predominate among the lakes and dales. Here nature seldom needs a second bidding to fill the crevices, once a little detritus borne of wind and rain, has provided the necessary anchorage for the germinating seedling. Ferns, stonecrops and navelwort abound in such conditions and to complete the picture from time to time an indigenous rose or the common bramble soon prostrate their lanky stems overall and command closer attention when in flower or fruit.

Alpine enthusiasts less content with leaving all to Mother Nature, will embark upon a planned course of development, poking some choice Tyrolean native into a likely niche with an added handful of compost to underpin success. Here again the world is the enthusiast's oyster with the usual limitations of time, space and perhaps a pocket of adequate depth.

2
Planting

Attention to the finer points of planting is undoubtedly the surest rock on which to build. Many a languishing plant exhibiting all manner of trace element deficiencies in later life may often be recorded as having been given an indifferent send off.

Conditions at the base of walls, especially those of a house, are often far from ideal for the satisfactory development of a good root system. I am convinced that thorough preparation and assistance in the formative years makes all the difference between success and a mediocre result or even complete failure.

The majority of deciduous planting is done in the winter months when the ground is at its wettest. The prudent gardener will therefore avoid preparing the planting site until the plants, of whatever ilk, are to hand. To prepare even a day earlier may well create a problem with waterlogged or hard-frozen conditions. Such breaking of the surface disturbs the natural capillaries and so retains moisture or frost to such an extent that the planting may well have to be abandoned. Undisturbed soil will always take far heavier downpours without materially affecting the structure than that broken up in advance, even weeks earlier. The less hardy subjects will have been grown under cover. Accordingly May is recommended as the safe planting time. In some seasons the end of the month or even June may be more prudent.

Preparation
Ready for the occasion the wise planter with the charges to hand, or rather tucked nicely away from dehydrating wind in plastic bag or like cover, if bare rooted, will have a ready supply of bone meal during winter operations. Spring and summer plantings are best accompanied with a blended fish, blood and bone fertiliser or an inorganic one such as Growmore. A sizeable bucketful of very well decayed manure, compost, leaf mould or fine bark will prove advantageous especially in hungry sands or conversely in heavy clays to assist in aeration and gradual break down by the humus content. A word of caution here insofar that with the possible exception of manure and bark the others are most likely to prove alkaline, so must be avoided when dealing with ericaceous material. For those, moss peat is unquestionably the ideal though viewed from this point may well be consigned to history before the present century is very far advanced. If it's to be peat then it must be the moss type from compressed bales. Most other offerings are of sedge peat which can actually prove alkaline. Ensure that it is always well moistened prior to application.

It may also help to fix the supports to the wall at this stage particularly where the shrub to be planted is quite large and might be damaged by the fixing process after planting *(see picture right)*. Commence by marking a semi-circle of about 60-90cm (2-3ft) in diameter depending upon the plant size, from the wall or fence. Where there is a great overhang of eave this may be increased, better larger than a niggardly attempt. Skim off any turf, laying carefully to one side, or if gravel remove entirely. Next dig out the top spit, spade's depth, to the side. Attention should then be turned to the lower spit breaking it up with a fork to its full measure and adding a generous amount of bone meal or Growmore along with the humus forming material *(see picture right)*. Working close to the footings of a house all manner of objects tend to surface including bricks, large stones and clods of clay. While the worst offenders are best removed there is little point in getting paranoid over its condition, in fact in some cases this detritus may assist with the drainage and aeration allowing the roots to break through to the surrounding soil. Return

some soil to the lower level, treading to consolidate and then replace the turf, a valuable sponge and source of rich humus which will quickly be colonised by fresh new roots. It matters little whether or not the turf is laid upside down, as some prefer. The hole may then be backfilled adding a further dressing of fertiliser.

So much for the near counsel of perfection on planting. Unfortunately short cuts have to be made from time to time where conditions are especially difficult, such as restriction of room, either breadth or depth. But cut corners at your peril for a large purse may then be spent attending an ailing duck whose illness could have been avoided in the first place.

An ever increasing number of our plants are nowadays supplied as containerised items - a subtle difference to container grown. The bottom line meaning that they may not have been so containerised for long and may well provide a problem at planting if, as sometimes happens, all the compost departs from the roots. Roses seem to be particularly affected along with some other deciduous subjects.

On the other hand clematis and most evergreens have always been grown throughout in containers and are unlikely to pose a problem; however the procedure is the same, keeping an alert eye should problems arise at the planting time.

Positioning

Many failures with wall shrubs are, without much doubt, due to over-close planting. Poking small plants into crevices may be alright on a dry wall or in the rock garden but not for any degree of permanency against house or garden wall. Walls act like sponges absorbing surrounding moisture and dispersing it throughout their structure and constantly drying out the surrounding soil, a position aggravated further at the base of one which is north-facing due to the much less frequent precipitation from that direction. No subject should be set closer than 25cm (10in), with half as far again for bushier subjects of modest vigour, more still for some. Overgenerous eaves are another factor especially of a bungalow where their proximity to the ground further reduces the available rainfall.

Containerised plants should be carefully knocked out of their pots by placing a hand over the surface and inverting over a spade handle, given a sharp tap to the pot rim, having first ensured that the compost has been well moistened then delivery should be prompt. If undue resistance is noted then slit the pot down one side and peel off. With large or heavy specimens this is invariably the best route to take, slitting both sides and using as handles to ease into position. Other than root balled specimens, never set a plant with any of the so called bio-degradable covers despite suppliers' claims. Root balled specimens require particular consideration, it being vital that the benefit of root balling is retained. To remove it *in toto*

6

before introducing it to the hole is likely to ensure its demise. On taking out an adequate hole with ample clearance, set the plant at the correct depth and untie or cut away the knots and lay the material flat. This may be hessian or jute or more likely acrylic mesh. The former will rot in a trice while the acrylic will prove little hindrance to newly forming roots. If particularly concerned the excess may be cut away though in no way disturbing the soil adhering to the roots. Backfill and tread firmly around but very lightly overhead where only the merest covering of soil should be given. A further firming around and overhead two or three weeks later should prove advantageous. Planting depth is critical. Better plant shallow than deep as roots will quickly penetrate to lower levels in the natural quest for moisture while at the same time assimilating nitrogen from the air. This is likely to be in short supply when cover is excessive. As a general guide 25-50mm (1-2in) should be the maximum over the topmost roots. Known stem rooters may on occasion be set slightly deeper. Many of our shrubs and particularly roses are budded or grafted on to more vigorous growing rootstocks which in turn frequently sprout new growth which can quickly overpower the selected variety. Accordingly the experienced gardener will ensure that the point of union is just visible. Some roses and viburnums are frequent offenders needing a constant vigil with prompt removal of root stock suckers on sight. It was often advised to plant clematis much deeper than hitherto so ensuring that the preferred variety developed its own rooting system rather than relying on that of the wild *C. vitalba*. Today virtually all are now grown on their own roots, thus the edict no longer holds sway. A similar recommendation applies also to tree paeonies which are grafted onto *P. officinalis*. Fortunately this seldom if ever attempts to overtake its new found host and so the original dictum still stands. Firmness is the order of the day on returning the soil. Ensure that it is well compacted around the root ball and over the top though only the merest sprinkle should be deposited, just enough to hide the original. Often the particular condition obtaining at the time will determine what action is required

If wet and pasty it is better to be less severe but return in two or three weeks time to complete the task, particularly if hard frost intervenes. Under dry conditions apply a thorough soaking, repeating about a week or ten days later when a generous mulch should be applied and then no further watering while the soil remains moist under the mulch. Many a casualty occurs from over-enthusiastic watering. Staking will vary according to the subject. In some cases a stout pressure treated cane should be inserted just prior to planting while in other cases a single bamboo will suffice and may best be placed afterwards to enable easier positioning against the wall. Fan trained specimens will on the other hand require several supports and the growths tied in. One refinement would be to give some protection to spindly growths of plants such as clematis which are always vulnerable to excited animals, human or otherwise. More information on tying and training will be found on the chapter dealing with this paramount aspect of furnishing walls and fences. Not all material will arrive in containers. Some will be bare rooted and delivered in a suitably sized plastic sack with a modicum of straw to preserve the roots against drying out and to protect against frost. Chief among these will be tree-size specimens, fruit and roses. Preparation of the site will follow the same course though perhaps rather more expansively, with the top spit awaiting final return until the correct depth has been tested and adjusted accordingly. Again the aim is to ensure that the topmost roots are kept close to the envisaged surface. At the same time determine the position and if possible insert staking as necessary. Under no circumstances should roots be coiled into the hole. In nearly every instance it is necessary to trim back all bare roots, limiting their length to a maximum of 60cm (2ft) overall. Many, including roses will profit from half that expanse. The crux of the matter is simply that inevitably on lifting, virtually every root end is severed, many much closer to the stock. A clean near surgical cut will quickly foster the development of a foraging fibrous root matt so underpinning quick establishment.

At the same time equalising their length as far as possible will assist in all-round anchorage. One further refinement is to check for signs of sucker activity while still handling the plant and if present tear away rather than cutting which will merely serve to increase the problem. Such cutting can never remove the tiniest of dormant growth buds that cluster around the base. (See chapter on Pruning.)

Should the roots show any sign of dehydration then a prompt dunking for ten or so minutes is necessary. Endeavour to set on a slight cone and make sure as far as possible that they radiate to all points of the compass. This is often a tricky operation. It should be borne in mind that the prime function of roots is to anchor, sustenance following to a greater or lesser degree depending upon the first criteria. I have found that the use of a small peg or wire staple, even a heavy stone will assist in positioning wayward roots to ensure that the subject is buttressed against wind from whichever quarter it chooses to blow.

Infilling takes the form of gently returning the top spit around the roots, treating each layer in turn so that they are set precisely at their original level and not carelessly battened down out of character. If there is any evidence of clodding, dispense with the soil removed and trickle in some finer material often to hand from a hedge bottom if no other supply such as an old Gro-bag is available. Once out of sight the final cover may come from the original soil and discretion used in firming. The majority of plants demand a firm root run and it may well prove necessary to return some days later if conditions were not totally ideal after an initial gentle treading home. As with container planting no more than 5cm (2in) should cover the topmost roots and the surface of this should be left loose to avoid cracking and assist with the necessary aeration.

Planting is a rather laborious process requiring strict attention to detail and yet an exciting time, giving birth as it may prove to be a long association with an especially chosen prodigy. If successful it will provide great pleasure in the ensuing years.

Special Considerations

Permanent paving means that planting in tubs or containers of varying styles and sizes is sometimes the only hope of growing shrubs in the microclimate of a wall. I am often asked if roses or clematis will grow in such circumstances; the reply being a guarded yes. Few will suffer such constrictions that the container imparts for more than two or three years. In some cases that figure may be doubled though few will prosper for much longer. While growth appears healthy and in accordance with the nature of the plant one may well push to the optimum period. I would generally favour such plantings as being rather temporary with a view to re-stocking after two or three years, planting the originals in the garden with a fifty-fifty chance of survival. Stone or concrete containers along with substantial oak or teak ones would prove the most reliable. Even then in very severe winters they may freeze solid which would sign the death certificate of most subjects. Few plants will tolerate their roots being frozen solid even though the tops will show little ill from such an extreme until later. Conversely overheating in the summer may prove equally harmful in varying ways, such as creating too dry a root run and so pre-disposing towards mildew attack, a known cause of such trouble.

Ericaceous Subjects

With ericaceous and known lime-haters a wise precaution, even before selecting the items, would be to make a soil test. This is a simple operation even for the absolute novice. Kits are available from most garden centres at a reasonable cost. The prime rules to follow are to sample very small quantities of soil from just below the surface in several locations. These are allowed to air dry over a few days without any skin contact. Each individual sample may be tested, or the overall mix, which is trickled into a phial and treated with the reactor fluid, thoroughly shaken and allowed to settle for ten or so minutes. The resultant colour change is then compared with the chart provided. Ph values below 7.0 are acidic, above 7.0 are alkaline.With ph 7 as the neutral point the most satisfactory for the widest range of plants, a lower reading even down to ph 4 will prove most suitable for lime-haters. The scale is logarithmic, any point change being ten times greater or lesser as the case involves.

It is perhaps surprising, though very welcome, that while lime-haters will not tolerate any degree of alkalinity lime lovers will somehow not only put up with supposedly hostile acid conditions but usually give a very good return. This rather underlines the point that it is seldom wise to apply lime other than in the vegetable patch, lest a revamp of the plot requires a lime-free medium. In such cases a generous application of moss peat that seems only to come in compressed bales, being about the most acid material to hand will greatly assist in delivering the desired conditions. Fortunately with the distinct possibility of political correctness, for what it is worth, the finer grades of forest bark may prove equally effective as peat is phased out. Chemicals offering a similar result, though lacking the humus content, include sulphate of ammonia, aluminium sulphate, ammonium nitrate and sulphur which should be the first consideration and used at about a heaped tablespoonful per square metre (sq yd) the others being used with much more discretion. Other substrates will in all probability emerge as the peat debate gathers momentum. As a belt and braces tactic the occasional use of Sequestrene, which supplies iron in a chelated form, is able to release the necessary iron which is locked up by the presence of lime, may well prove beneficial. The preparation Miraclegrow makes a similar claim with the advantage of a high nitrogen content calculated to give a quick boost to growth. They have their uses and may help to deliver the right response, though not overnight. Another ploy in defying nature is to make up raised beds, very much a current vogue, filled with soil of known acidity, after overlaying the original surface with a plastic sheet to prevent the capillary movement of underlying alkaline moisture. In laying the sheeting ensure that free drainage is permitted all round. Such constructions will clearly demand more attention to watering in dry periods.

While the dormant season from November to March is without doubt the best period to move or plant deciduous subjects, thanks to the garden centres the majority of trees, shrubs and herbaceous plants are available every day of the year. The prudent gardener will still prefer the dormant period but some may still wish to plant at other times even if only as in-fillers or where a failure has occurred. Only the foolhardy would try to plant in conditions of hard frost or when the ground is waterlogged or sun-baked. The latter being more easily dealt with by first thoroughly soaking the whole area a day or so beforehand, assuming that the baking has dried out the land. After planting, a thorough soaking and a heavy mulch will materially assist in establishment while an added gesture would be to lightly spray overhead as the sun goes down. A comparable cooling shower for the plant before one enjoys a similar refresher. Shielding with Netlon shade material or something similar may give relief to stress in the early days.

3
Mulching and Feeding

Mulching

Next to planting mulching must be regarded as the most critical factor in the successful cultivation of trees and shrubs. The aim is to form a blanket over the supposed root area for the immediate future, so largely preventing the soil capillaries from losing moisture gleaned from lower levels into the hands of ever warming sunshine and leeching winds, a process responsible for the greatest loss of residual water.

Whereas spring is often recommended as the preferred time to apply, following the winter rains, a much earlier application will have the added benefit of protecting the surface feeding roots from excessively low temperatures. Very few of our general plants benefit from frozen roots, a point highlighted when the very hard frosts of the 1980s took their toll of vast quantities of camellias, hollies and viburnums languishing in containers on raised garden centre tables, a factor largely overlooked in the past.

Provided the soil is well moistened then the sooner that mulching is carried out after autumn planting the better.

Mulching materials are almost endless. Those that break down into humus and gradually supplement the residual plant food, in addition to improving the crumb structure of the surface soil are preferable, but inert materials certainly have their place.

Lawn mowings

Usually the most readily available and certainly not to be despised provided they are applied quite thinly, evenly and with repetitive dressings. The exception is following the use of systemic weed-killers for about the first three mowings. The vapourisation of the chemicals may, just may, affect soft newly emerging growth near to the ground. A cautious approach that is worth implementing is by using the mowings on the compost heap or digging into vacant ground.

To safeguard against any scorching of tender shoots arising from soil level apply just the merest dressing at that point, thickening towards the perimeter. It is quite suitable for all subjects.

Garden compost

This is the next most likely material on hand and provided that it has been well made so that the injurious weed seeds and any persistent root stocks have been eliminated, then it is first class material. A more generous spread with up to 75mm (3in) at the outside and again slightly dishing close to the subject is acceptable. More likely than not this will be alkaline and so unsuitable for ericaceous plants.

Manure

Without doubt this is the counsel of perfection though becoming increasingly difficult to obtain. It is more likely to be ericaceous friendly giving a neutral to acid reaction. Ideally applied slightly thicker than compost.

Whereas one would balk at using fresh manure when planting, using it as a mulch will maximise its fertiliser value rather than allow it to be leeched by incessant rains while waiting in the wings until it has become well rotted. Just avoid close contact with newly emerging shoots.

Leaf mould

Had pride of place prior to the advent of peat on the grand scale. When made from beech or oak and used after a twelve month break-down has few equals and should be suitable for ericaceous plants. Made from most other broad-leaved trees it is likely to prove alkaline and while admirable for most, caution will be needed with lime-haters. Little chance of any scorching of tender shoots and so best applied generously.

Peat

Universally recommended until the recent concerns of the conservationists over excessive extraction and loss of endemic flora and fauna. Likely to become much less available. For that good reason its use should be reserved for the azaleas, rhododendrons, camellias and other lime-haters. Some advantage may be gained in deterring slugs by applying generously close up to succulent stems when using moss peat, which has a ph value of 4.5 to 5. Sedge peat may prove alkaline.

Bark

A one time throw-away waste material, bark has become a major player with a wide range of uses in the garden. From an ornamental point it has few equals and certainly makes a first class mulching material. While the food value is minimal its useful life exceeds most other materials, even the finest ground will last up to two years while the coarsest grades will easily persist for twice that period. All grades being suitable for most plants though the ph will be variable with pine bark registering about ph 6; woodchips tending to prove more alkaline.

Cocoashell

A newcomer to the field, though seeming to be expensive, will give at least three year's service, needing to be applied 50 to 75mm (2-3in) thick.

Gravel

This more or less has to be the obvious choice in a patio situation rather than something the birds are forever disturbing. Where possible the ideal would be to be to apply a humus-forming material topped with stone. A good depth will retain moisture well.

Others

Local industries produce a variety of waste products such as leather trimmings, shoddy, coffee bean husks and cinnamon bark peelings. I've found these by-products of the essential oils industry first class. Mushroom compost or rather the spent version is much in evidence in some localities. Its shortcoming is its high calcium content not much use for the ericaceous tribe.

Feeding

The first three years after planting are critical in establishing all trees and shrubs. During this period most will return a better dividend if their food supply is enhanced by a positive programme of additional supplements. Apply according to their supposed needs as to whether sluggish growth needs bolstering or soft sappy shoots are in need of hardening prior to the onset of winter or perhaps extra nutrients for berry and fruit production. Principal amongst these are -

Bone Meal

Since time immemorial this has been the accepted standby as a long term slow release and organic fertiliser. Applied during autumn and winter principally when planting, or as a top-up later in life. It provides a small amount of nitrogen to promote growth with a much larger percentage of phosphate for the encouragement of added root development. It has the virtue of being quite harmless to root and shoot on contact and is usefully applied as several generous 'gloved' handfuls, over the supposed root run.

Hoof and Horn Meal.

Another slow acting fully organic fertiliser with a much higher nitrogen content than bone meal reflected in its pricing. Used in much the same manner.

Blood Fish and Bone
Combining three organics to provide a long term slow release with a more rapid acting nitrogenous fertiliser. Best used from April onwards when planting and as a surface dressing lightly hoed in or mulched over.

Dried Blood.
A rapid-acting organic form of nitrogen, which should be applied and well watered. Most effective from April to June.

Sulphate of Ammonia.
The standard quick-acting inorganic form of nitrogen. May be applied from late March until June. Avoid contact with plant tissue to which it is caustic. It has an acidifying effect on the soil. Water thoroughly after applying.

Bonfire Ash.
A rich form of potash if gathered from freshly felled timber. Must be kept dry to avoid leeching from rain. Likely to increase the alkalinity of most soils. Spring use most effective.

Sulphate of Potash.
An often recommended inorganic requirement for successful fruit growing and as an aid to hardening soft tissue so helping to promote ripening and flower development. Best applied in late winter. Scatter as a modest dusting.

Sulphate of Iron.
Used to increase soil acidity and improve foliage colour. Applied in solution or as a light dressing during the growing season.

Growmore.
This is the standard inorganic general fertiliser for application during the growing season. Water well after spreading, at manufacturer's recommended rate.

Osmacote. This is the inorganic slow release alternative to Bone and Hoof and Horn. May be applied at any time though usually in spring.

Liquid Growth Stimulants. These are applied during the main growing season, often of high nitrogen to boost growth. Others are specifically targeted at mineral deficiencies. Frequently recommended as foliar feeds through their ability to improve foliage colour and counteract supposed shortcomings. I have yet to see leaves that have lost their initial lustre show much improvement if any. More likely their effect is noted in newly emerging leaves. Chief among these is Miracid, Sequestrene and the several seaweed based products such as Maxicrop. Stick rigidly to the manufacturer's recommendations when applying.

Polymers. Not a growth stimulant in the strict sense but indirectly and of much value under dry conditions. Coming as tiny granules capable of absorbing up to eighty times their volume with water releasing it gradually to the drier surrounding soil and recharging when next soaked.
Either sprinkle into the planting hole or mix with water to produce a frog-spawn-like substance into which the bare roots should be dunked.

4
Pruning

Few topics are more calculated to excite the would-be planter than the requirements of pruning. Give a friend a plant and I'll warrant that one of the first three questions posed relates to the intricacies of pruning. Based upon the all too common fallacy that pruning a plant is either necessary or beneficial and likely to forthwith increase its floriferousness. Nothing of course could be further from the truth. Pruning is a national habit, a fetish and a consistent subject of conversation down at the local and surely the best place for getting it out of the system. In fact the golden rule should always be – don't unless absolutely necessary.

The great con surrounds the premise that cutting back a plant will somehow induce the remainder to produce a super abundance of flowers where hitherto it was barren. In practice this only holds good in certain very controlled circumstances, notably trained fruit. Even then while the miracle may seem to have been performed one has actually reduced the number of potential fruit buds to the detriment of the remaining leaf buds which it is hoped will become transformed in a trice rather than the scheduled time normally taken. Hard cutting back reduces the many to the advantage of the few but in most cases excites unproductive shoots at the expense of bloom.

A typical shoot of cotoneaster or peach produced in a season say of 40cm (15in) length, will, if left alone, continue onwards the following year to about the same length and at the same time push out one or two side shoots from near the base of the original part. A sequence which will continue ad infinitum, the secondary shoots in turn sending out their sub-laterals. The axilliary buds formed in the first year, between leaf stalk and stem, will flower in the next year. Some genera require an additional twelve months for the transition, of which apples and pears are typical examples.

Now if, instead of leaving our initial growth alone, the secateurs are brought into play, depending upon how far the shoot was decapitated, clearly, a number of flower buds would be scotched and the remaining buds forced into strong shoot growth. By lightly cutting back, say one quarter, one would tend to get the best of both worlds by encouraging some new growths, yet not stimulating the plant so much as to force all the remaining buds to forge ahead. On the other hand if three quarters is taken away then virtually every bud left will push out and all the flowers will have been cut off. This is a logical process of a plant endeavouring to re-establish its natural balance twixt root and shoot. In growth there is perfect harmony, displace either part and the other seeks to make amends. Additionally another contingency arises and that is the time at which such operations are carried out. A bare shoot that is lightly tipped immediately after leaf fall, or in the case of evergreens, before growth ceases, having lost its force for progress, immediately endow the next remaining bud and those successively down the shoot with additional energy to push forward when conditions are suitable.

A science degree is not needed to appreciate that, having all winter in which to fortify the next of kin bud, if this tip removal takes place at the end of the winter there will be panic in the system while resources are re-aligned. During this period much valuable growing time is lost at the commencement of spring growth. Such application is bedrock in the cultivation of intensively trained trees, shrubs and fruit.

Incessant tampering with the superstructure must inevitably weaken the root system, though initially the so overbalanced roots cause a rush of new stem growth. Nowhere is this better illustrated than with the popular pastime of making bush roses ape bedding plants. For the first ten years or so progress is good enough, but the roots tiring of the annual butchering gradually run out of steam in having to explore for food on an ever increasing arc and translocate it back to the stems, for root growth is an extension process rather than a rebirth of new material from the crown. Personal proof of this may be gained by digging up an old specimen of two score years and severely trimming all roots, such as they are, back to no more than 15cm (6in) in length. Well replanted it will be born again. Left alone from the start, although they would in many cases make unacceptably large specimens, certainly their life span would be greatly extended.

The wise gardener will then place more store on doing his homework for each and every individual plant, so that there is no requirement to squeeze quarts into pint pots and will train, tie-in and pinch out more growing tips rather than letting innermost sadistic motives take over in the mistaken belief that "it does 'em good".

As ever, rules are made to be broken and with the best of intentions, and despite much careful guidance, sooner or later some resort to the secateurs will be necessary. Breastwood is always a problem and the more so when the hope is to establish a floral skin to the house, rather than merely planting shrubs against its walls. After the needed branches have been duly tied-in the surplus should either be taken hard back to source or in some cases reduced to an obvious flower bud or spur near to the main stem. Yet again much of this may be obviated by deftly rubbing out precocious buds and shoots when growth commences and so eliminate later corrections.

The golden rule of shrub pruning should apply equally to those on walls and fences and that is to carry out the operation **immediately after flowering** except for those that bloom after mid-summer, they being dealt with the following spring. Evergreens in the main should similarly be cut back at the commencement of growth in spring while they may also have a secondary trim on completion at the end of summer. The one incontrovertible rule in any pruning exercise is always to cut to a bud. Such bud, or node is usually to be found lurking in the axil between leaf stalk, petiole and stem though not always and sometimes its presence may not be very obvious. Indeed as in the case of the latent buds near to the base of roses the format is little more than a barely discernible wrinkle, but given a close inspection an embryo bud may just be apparent. In this particular instance an even closer view will reveal sister buds on either side, which may be regarded as additional strings to one's bow in the event of damage. It will be clear that there is a diversity of appearance of latent buds so demanding all the care and precision so often spelt out. Furthermore it is imperative that cuts are always made fairly close to the bud. Not so close as to obviously rupture the tissue but sufficiently so to reduce to the minimum the internodal growth. This will be unable to develop further and will gradually die back to form an abscission layer above the bud though equally in the meanwhile disease could enter and may know no bounds.

One frequently repeated guide line to which I do not subscribe is that the cut should be slanted. In some case yes, such as when major limbs are being shorn off close to a trunk, or one is heading back a maiden, or single upright shoot to encourage lateral development and at the same time wish to obtain a continuance of the vertical growth without disfiguring the main stem. In this latter case a slight slope away from the bud may improve the final visual appearance. Furthermore should a knife be used, the only tool for pruning until the advent of secateurs, then you will have no choice but to make a slanting cut. Where secateurs are the preferred tool, 99.9 percent of the time clean straight cuts, the shortest distance between two points are usually preferable.

When dealing with large limbs, or for that matter other sizeable branches, always cut back to the point of intersection. The sight of unkempt stub ends is the emblem of the wood butcher and not for the gardener. Such severances should always be attended by a near clinical finish, paring the rind and outer heartwood with a really sharp knife such as the 'Stanley' or a chisel so removing the ragged tissue of the saw cut. Over the passing years various recommendations have been made to prevent infection of the open wound. A clear antiseptic known as Medo was first in the field supplanting the old habit of using up the bathroom paint to seal the cut.

Next on the market came Arbrex which is still available though now rather out of favour. Allegedly, it is held that manifestations of trouble are spawned unseen whereas a carefully trimmed surface will rapidly callous over, some doing so at a much faster rate than others. From time to time it will become apparent that a shrub has become, as we say in to-day's parlance, 'past its sell by date', in short crying out for a major attempt at regeneration. Some are ready partners in this while others may well not take kindly to the operation and would be the better if grubbed and replaced, though with a different genera or a full soil change. Alternatively just swapping places with another may often be the preferred way forward. Where severe cutting back is contemplated the accepted guide is to operate on the evergreens in early April, and the prudent gardener will ensure that some foliage is retained. Or, put another way, cut back no further than immediately above the lower cluster of foliage, so leaving a life line while the plant overcomes the trauma. Deciduous subjects offer a quite different picture insofar that if they are reduced while in complete dormancy, late November to early January they may with advantage be cut quite close to the ground. In response the buds, however latent, that remain, especially those near the top, will be fattening up over the remaining dormant period ready to burst forth when the call comes as the temperatures rise. A certain amount of careful thinning will often be required and some nursing of the strong unusually succulent shoots. Quite heroic growth is usually the order of the day in the plant's effort to return to its natural balance of root and shoot. The opposite part of the equation is that by such severe treatment being carried out in March or April many a plant will bleed to death due to the osmotic pressure from the moisture gathering roots excited by the rising temperatures.

Satisfactory pruning can only be carried out if the tools are all in pristine operating condition. Without fail whenever sallying forth to do some serious pruning, and surely all pruning is serious, spend a few seconds in buffing up the secateurs as mercifully my barber always strops his razor. A few strokes at some 20 degrees angle on either side of the Rolcut pattern or on one side only of the by-pass kinds, followed by a flat rub on its opposite face to clear the burr, is all that is required. Check over the saws ensuring that the all important set is correct, so making passage through wet wood easily accomplished. Rubbing both sides, with a candle will lubricate the most obstinate.

Root pruning

The other side of the coin to forever snipping at the branch-work is to address the problem of runaway growth where it begins, at the powerhouse out of sight below ground. Attention there will often prove much more rewarding than any detailed operation above. For many years wall plums and sweet cherries have been on the receiving end of such treatment due partly to their abhorrence of the knife, sometimes bringing gumming and die-back in its wake.

Simply pressing the spade to its full depth and a little extra shove at no more than 30cm (12in) distance from the trunk may well suffice for a first attempt after about two years. This will certainly drastically curtail the surface roots with usually a most salutary effect

A more serious matter with recalcitrant offenders would be to remove a trench at the same distance and the width of the spade and then explore the under-side, cutting cleanly through any thicker members making their way downwards. The operation over, the trench is back-filled, treading firmly and for good measure a thick mulch applied.

Now, that is more or less the format etched in stone for wall fruit. Why not then for the lazy rose, ceanothus, cotoneaster or any other subject that appears not to be giving a good return for the obvious TLC with which it is constantly bestowed? Likely to have more effect, I would suggest, than the oft recommended application of a handful of sulphate of potash.

Bark ringing

Another fruit ploy deemed to give similar results though taboo on stone fruits due to their tendency to gum, is ring barking *(see right)*. Little more than pressing a knife into the bark half way round the trunk and repeated 2cm (1in) lower will allow the bark to be peeled off. A similar rather shorter semi-circle is removed above or below on the opposite side with a resulting near complete girdling. Total encirclement would be likely to prove fatal in

some circumstances though sometimes this can be carried out given that the semi-circles are well spaced to permit cross-flow of sap.

Early April is the preferred timescale for this while full root pruning is best carried out during the latter months of the year. Its wider application on ornamentals may prove equally as positive and worth trying in stubborn cases of non-flowering. Who has not seen the effect of an overlooked tie that has resulted in a bonanza of blossom from checking the flow of sap?

Suckers

A number of wall plants are budded or grafted on to alien rootstocks ostensibly to provide a stronger rooting capacity than the particular subjects can provide. Often attributable to more highly bred variants than the common type. Indeed virtually all roses are so developed though one leading grower turned over to providing their entire listing on their own roots. Unfortunately, laudable though this exercise proved, sadly it failed to provide plants that appealed to the garden centre customers. Their somewhat miserable growth in the crucial first season drove to a re-think at source resulting in reverting to the traditional practice. In fact while they certainly looked poor specimens initially they made amends to good effect in subsequent years.

Plants on their own roots enjoy the great benefit of having emerging growths from below soil level taken as a bonus. Whereas any that arise from a budded or grafted one will immediately be viewed with suspicion and prudently removed lest it overtakes the apple of one's eye.

Removal must be effected by actually tearing away the shoot from its point of origin so removing the inherent basal buds lurking close to the main stem. Simply cutting, however close, will fail to remove these dormant eyes and the sucker problem will increase ad infinitum.

5
Training and Tying

The certain success of the majority of wall plants hinges on the diligent attention to careful training and securing, executed not in one fell swoop but over the entire growing season. To wait until a young growth, with the brittle vigour of summer's lushness, has overshot its mark and then in a hasty moment endeavour to bring it back within bounds, will surely bring catastrophe. Whereas an occasional check in its line of growth, or a tip removed will save many a tear at a later date. Most, perhaps aided with a temporary tie will respond to a little human assistance along the path to the perfection of form in the planter's eye. Often little more than a nudge to a wayward clematis shoot is all that is needed with the leaf stalk grasping its intended support in a trice.

Working on the principle, which as far as I am aware has not been debunked in these enlightened days, that the more vertical a shoot grows the more vigorous it becomes, much subsequent chin stroking may be saved by, wherever possible, bending it horizontally or even at times downward. Such a procedure is often applied in commercial orchards with the salutary effect of concentrating the sap flow into forming flower and fruit at the expense of shoot extension.

Alternative methods of fixing

Unfortunately walls and to a lesser degree fences are often the victims of damaging squalls fostered by other buildings and barriers, along with their own peculiar micro-climate. Unless abject despair is to reign with monotonous frequency, a truly reliable system capable of withstanding such trauma is necessary and at the same time it must appear unobtrusive.

The particular subject and local conditions will largely dictate which method to adopt. Stout growing shrubs such as pyracantha and ceanothus may need little more than an occasional tie to a vine eye, making a more substantial anchor than the old leaded nails.

Training

Wiring a wall

A full blown properly wired wall is the preferred system par excellence for the majority of subjects as witnessed at most leading gardens *(see picture right)*. Once set up it will last for decades and provide a continuous matrix of support and at the same time be scarcely noticeable. Generally the wires are set horizontally, or occasionally vertically to suit particular sites. The horizontal ones start at about 75cm (30in) above soil level with 15cm (6in) to 22cm (9in) spacing the latter chiefly for peaches and most fruit. Fixings are set at 3m (10ft) distances securing the wire only at the ends, the use of tensioners completing a professional job. Use only galvanised wire of 2mm gauge which will far outlive plastic.

Wire coils have a distinct mind of their own and until the knack of turning the coil as the length is paid out is acquired it often pays to lay it on the ground and draw off each required length retaining the remainder with a weight. Some may prefer to use the drift vine eyes which are usually quite suitable where old lime mortar applies, being readily knocked home. Drilling to accept the screwed version is not very satisfactory in such cases and so entry will be into the bricks. In the case of modern cement mortar it matters little either way. Most garden centres and stores stock screwed eyes, though at a price in small homogenised packs. Where a substantial quantity is required the builders' merchants should make it easier on the pocket. For general purposes 10cm (4in) No l2 size will be needed though No 10 gauge will suffice for small areas. Comparable sized Rawlplugs and a power drill with masonry bit completes the kit. Eyes of a shorter length are usually preferable when coping with individual branches as with a magnolia or pyracantha.

Trellis
Not always will a full-dress training system be required, the area perhaps being a small area twixt door and window. Here a format of 'S' double cross using six eyes and running the wire to form a double 'X' and a perimeter rectangle. Admirable for most clematis. Alternatively this is where the vertical system of parallel wires comes into play. More often I suspect the choice homes in for some form of stylised trellis of either wood or plastic. Whichever, always make sure that brass screws are used; expensive yes, but ensuring removal is child's play whenever demanded rather than coping with rusted iron ones firmly embedded.

Battens
Another form of wooden support is the use of battens in the manner of a giant square trellis, often seen on larger properties for training vigorous shrubs. Pressure treated wooden strips are screwed home at 15cm (6in) vertically, again using brass screws. These are then crossed at the same spacing. These proud laterals make for easier tying of strong branches.

Netting
Mainly for covering parapets or where disguising some ugly roof. There is a wide choice of materials which need a minimum of attachment. Pig, chain-link, and plastic all may play a part.

Fan training
This is the most satisfactory method for training especially for lax growers. The approach is to select from four upwards well-placed limbs that can be identified as forming the basis of a fan *(see picture right)*. Often there is a surplus of available material which permits the selection of those of more or less equal vigour and the removal of the also-rans. These are secured either directly to parallel wires or canes that in turn are similarly fastened. This is most effective if the growths are too willowy. The centre should be kept open with the outer growths fastened as low as possible. As these and others that develop in the middle come to the end of their permitted run  they are stopped back. The more vigorous may be cut back to a lower lateral which in turn will assume the leadership. In stopping back, a mere pinch of the growing point will often do little more than excite the bud immediately below, which will forge ahead as if nothing had happened. Make therefore a generous reduction of at least a hand's breadth. With further development, shoots will grow outwards and where these are likely to be unwanted, pinching back as they arise will help to maintain control. A degree of bushiness will be the aim in many cases while still retaining the original pattern. In such cases pruning back to preserve the form should be carried out straight after flowering, with certain exceptions such as wall fruit. In that case it is done after harvesting.

Tying

One of the most significant details of maintaining a wall in full power is the somewhat mundane operation of tying, yet upon its diligent application everything depends. How often one encounters the ligatured limb, caused by either the use of wrong materials or most frequently by tying too tightly in the first instance and failing to carry out a regular inspection. No ties should ever be considered as permanent, but merely of annual duration. Although some will last considerably longer, this often creates a false sense of security and that is where the danger lies. Annual stem girth expands out of all proportion in wet seasons and unless frequently monitored the slack is taken up and the over-tight tie acts as a tourniquet with an inbuilt mission to strangle and the production of unwanted reassertive shoots *(see picture right)*. Always leave sufficient room to insert a thumb.

For most purposes tarred string is the ideal material. Unfortunately this is one of those familiar aids to gardening which seems to have been swept away, doubtless for some obscure reason, though a trip to a ship's chandler may prove otherwise. Generally available are standard balls that have been treated with some preservative which at least should hold for a good twelve-month. Bass and untreated fillis have little application, furthermore the gaudy spools of nylon string, along with wire, must be avoided like the plague. Who has not used these to their everlasting sorrow? The packs of short wire ties are acceptable only as a temporary measure and should be coiled, never ever twisted.

Labelling

Few aspects of gardening can be more exasperating than that of labelling. The discerning will surely wish to have their charges legibly labelled even though they may well be blessed with encyclopaedic minds, that at a bidding can rattle off some lengthy epithet in a latinised format. Others of less academic ability will depend upon the prompting label to underpin their interest and come to the rescue when proudly displaying their charges to friends of similar interest.

Such is the ongoing problem of finding a fail-safe system that will stand up to the vagaries of the weather and the predations of animal life in the widest context. This has produced a veritable arsenal of supposedly ideal systems, but few have survived. Without hesitation having travelled the road with all its trials just three have survived. Pride of place must go to the engraved botanic type as used by Kew and Wisley. Rather expensive though seemingly indestructable under garden conditions and readily observed at a modest distance. These are usually affixed to short aluminium stems or nailed direct on to a trunk with copper nails and a buffering spring. Alternatively a more substantial effect comes with their being nailed on to pressure-treated short stakes of 25mm (1in) square. Again copper roofing nails obtainable from a builders' merchant should be used. The label suppliers readily pre-drilling as desired.

Next on the list are the aluminium tags unfortunately not generally available in garden centres, more's the pity, but frequently advertised in the garden press and at most RHS shows. Their very simplicity is a joy indeed for marked with an ordinary HB pencil they will remain legible for twenty years. Corrections however are well nigh impossible though they do have two sides

Lastly to the ubiquitous plastic type reminiscent of the old wooden ones whitened on one side. For a short term the plastics are fine, again using an HB pencil. Furthermore they are readily cleaned with one of the modern detergents their demise usually due to the absorption of ultra violet light and inevitable brittleness.

While both the aluminium and plastic ones may be affixed to a stake more usually they would be hung on to a nearside branchlet using essentially either lead or copper wire. More than ample slack should be left to allow for annual growth, or as is so often the case several years growth before checking. Set in a wire loop, while proving acceptable and safer from the ligature hazard, it is more useful for lowly subjects than shrubs.

Protection

By definition many of the subjects selected for growing against walls and fences are of a less hardy constitution than the majority of our normal plantings. In the open border their lifespan would be precarious or a dismal failure. Against a wall they have an infinitely better chance of survival and with some added protection their successful cultivation is often assured. Some are merely at risk from late spring frosts while others will not tolerate winter temperatures more than a degree or so below freezing. Up to minus 2C (28F) can usually be kept at bay in a late spring frost by the use of fleece or the thicker terram as used in road and path building.

This is useful in the case of camellias and pieris that flower early. Further the frosts are only of short duration while winter cold spells may go on for days and in so doing will take their toll of the particularly sensitive specimens. Additional to the fleece, bubble polythene will prove helpful while interleaving branches with bracken or straw will add a further dimension. Protection at ground level of the basal parts will often save an otherwise vulnerable plant which will regenerate from the soil level.

6
Propagation

Increasing one's stock is always a fascinating and endlessly interesting business. The more prudent will automatically give serious thought to the gentle art on receipt of some new acquisition, expensive or otherwise, if nothing more than to act as an insurance lest some ill befalls the plant.

Whether green fingers or not enter the equation is debatable. More likely it is that the student will adhere to the recommended route while the casual gardener will just pop in a slip and be demoralised when failure stares one in the face. As the greatest majority of wall plants are either distinct species or selected forms the customary route to mass increase, namely seed, seldom applies. Even so when the chance arises along with the necessary gift of patience then let the enthusiast go for gold. There is always the chance of a world beater being discovered. In lottery terms 'Just Maybe'.

Seed

Should be collected when fully ripe, cleaned and stored in a fridge at a temperature about one degree above freezing. Some, such as eccremocarpus, will be required to be sown in heat in spring at 21C (70F) and lightly covered. Kept shaded from direct sun and pricked out as soon as handleable. Subsequently moved to a cold frame in small pots and finally planted out when sufficiently developed. This may be in June or perhaps held over to the following year.

Other seed such as pyracantha will need to be sown in trays using one of the standard composts or John Innes No. 1 with one third additional coarse grit added, just covering the seed from view, and positioning against a north-facing wall to over-winter. Prudence will dictate a further cover of wire netting as a foil to birds, cats and the like. Germination would be expected by April when the usual procedures of pricking out, potting and growing on in a cold frame should follow. Planting out may not be a viable proposition for two or more years. Alternatively, settle in a well prepared nursery bed.

Layering

For the many shrubs that lend themselves to this form of increase this is clearly the easiest, replicating in every detail all the good points of the parent and unfortunately all the bad ones. Autumn is the preferred time though little or no rooting will commence before the following late spring. It has the advantage of settling in the branchlet and avoiding the chances of damaging newly emerging apical growth.

The format is to select a flexible branch of modest proportions as near to the ground as possible. Remove all the foliage likely to be buried. Some advocate cutting into the stem just below a node and then upwards to the next one, or further, to form a tongue. A hole is then trowelled out as required about 10cm (4in) deep and filled with a mix of half peat and half sand, burying the layer half-way down. The end shoot is then tied to a small cane as upright as possible. The compost is firmed and for good measure a brick or stone placed over, so assisting in moisture retention and securing the finished job. For my part I have long since dispensed with cutting a tongue merely laying in the branch but at the same time kinking it as much as possible. Cane and stone still a necessary adjunct.

Air layering

Air layering is sometimes brought into play particularly with magnolias where there is a dearth of suitably placed lower branches. The form is to firstly fasten a splint to the selected shoot which should be about the thickness of a finger, then cut into the stem just below a leaf joint and upwards to the next one. Slightly prise open the tongue and holding a handful of damp moss around the cut section tease a strand or so into the wound and then bind with clear polythene, securing at each end.

Two years will usually be required before strong root activity is noted at which point detach and pot firmly and grow on under cover until sufficiently developed for final planting.

Hardwood cuttings

These are next in line for ease of plant increase. Little more than a sheltered corner with some amelioration of the soil is necessary. Cuttings may be taken from mid-September until the year's end with a bias to the earlier date. They should be about 20cm (8in) in length, the thickness of a pencil and taken from the current season's ripened growth. Any flowers or buds should be removed along with all but the two topmost leaves. In some cases, such as roses, all foliage is best stripped off.

Prepare a slit trench 8cm (3in) wide and 25cm (10in) deep. Three quarters fill with a fifty-fifty mix of peat and sharp sand. Trim squarely immediately below a leaf joint and insert to leave the two leaves just proud of the surface and firm up. The more that is buried the more likely will they root, in fact one leaf showing in a long jointed subject would be adequate. If successful new growth will begin to show in April or early May. All that remains is to ensure that no ill befalls the prodigies before lifting in the autumn. Much care is then required especially with roses, which only root from the very base, to ensure that the entire root system is lifted intact. In some cases the new acquisitions may be placed in their final resting place or lined out to develop into more substantial plants.

An alternative is to set the cuttings in pots of the same compost formula and stand in a cold frame with the pots plunged to their rims, so avoiding total freezing should the winter prove exceptionally severe. Often more suitable for evergreens.

Semi-hardwood

Here the material is just as described; the lower part well ripened while the tip is still in growth. These are generally removed with a heel, a sliver of the older wood, as they are eased away. Often however they will be just straight cuttings of short jointed habit and minus the heel. Mostly a matter of personal taste. Availability extends from early summer to autumn; the later and often more ripened cuttings may be placed in a cold frame using similar compost to that already described. Earlier in the year the use of a heated propagator *(see picture on right)* often proves a means to a quicker return. Whether with a heel or not pieces no more than 8cm (3in) in length are the ideal with the lower leaves removed with one or at most two at the tip. Again shoots devoid of flower are required and if the tip is particularly soft it may be nipped off without loss of impetus and subsequent development. See Softwood Cuttings for a fuller description of the propagator.

Softwood cuttings

There is no close season for the taking of softwood cuttings as such, though in practice there will be few opportunities or desirability for action in mid-winter. Pieces no more than 8cm (3in) in length and about two thirds the thickness of a pencil are taken, preferably from side growths rather than the long jointed over-soft apical shoots. They are carefully removed with a razor blade, cutting immediately below a leaf joint and the lower leaves removed. Sometimes the blade is also best used here lest the cutting joint is torn away in the leaf removal.

Some, notably clematis, root better from internodal cuttings prepared by severing between the leaf joints and trimming back above the pair of leaves to make a letter 'T' about 75mm (3in) overall. Dip in hormone rooting powder to assist in developing an earlier and more vigorous rooting system, though it has little effectiveness on subjects that are proven non-rooters. Using the previously recommended compost gently press the cuttings in for just over a quarter of their length. This ensures that the all important base is firmly in contact with the medium, dibbling in would not ensure this.

The propagator will require heating from $16^{\circ}C$-$21^{\circ}C$ ($60^{\circ}F$-$70^{\circ}F$) a temperature that can only be obtained if the house is itself warmed to within 4-$5^{\circ}C$ (8-$10^{\circ}F$) of that figure. Trying to raise the required temperature in an unheated structure is a non-starter. Heat is all important and with higher temperatures comes higher humidity. After placing the pots, water and then mist overhead. While further waterings should not be needed until rooting takes place, misting will need to be a continual procedure. On occasions lift the cover to check for over humidity and for any incidence of disease. The whole apparatus requires a north light position. If such is unavailable then some form of shading such as fleece or even newspaper should be brought into play in direct bursts of sun. Once rooting is evident by freshening of the tip with new leaves beginning to emerge, the cuttings should be potted singly and then returned for several days until on examination fresh roots have begun to emerge through the compost.

Thereafter into a weaning case nearby, which can be lidded over if required and serve as a home until they are ready for the cold frame.

7
Pests and Diseases of Ornamentals

It is customary in such a work to include a chapter on the sundry pests and diseases likely to be encountered. This is very laudable and it so happens that when I made the first draft of this book I included that provision; that was 20 years ago and much water has since flowed under the bridge of time.

Today some chemicals that have proved their worth and for the most part had little if any deleterious effect, have been ruled out of order. Those being retained have a limited permitted use only. Though the product may despatch aphids very successfully on roses because it does not have official approval for use against the same quarry on cabbages then it is proscribed. In legal jargon that would be called 'off label use' and strictly forbidden though the practicalities of this rather stretch the imagination.

As I understand, the garden centre market for many chemicals is minuscule compared to industry and it does not make financial sense to waste time and materials producing small packages when much larger ones can be shifted far more quickly. So we have items being withdrawn solely on financial marketing ploys.

In this climate of considerable flux it would seem pointless to specify particular chemicals, rather to identify the problem and leave you dear reader to seek up to date advice from the Royal Horticultural Society or one of the many agro/horticultural colleges. Fortunately as will be seen from the text the majority of wall plants are remarkably free from the arsenal of pests and diseases that deploy from time to time. Roses it would seem are the most vulnerable with a legion of possible ailments, surprising how they remain so popular in such adversity. That said while many will appear to be completely trouble free, on occasion some rogue predator or blight descends and while causing distress at the time may be looked upon as just one of those things and unlikely to recur.

Much publicity is given to the use of natural predators and introduced biological controls. Unfortunately the biological ones used under glass do not work outside due to the low temperature especially at night. We are then left with the ladybirds, ichneumon flies, sundry beetles and other members of the great insect world on which we must pin our faith and do all in our power to encourage them where possible. Birds and in particular blue tits have an insatiable lust for aphids especially greenfly, so much so that for the first time in my gardening career I am delighted at the continuous infestation that occurs on the flower stalks of Abutilon 'Kentish Belle', their contortions at feeding time keep the Pearce household much amused. Strange that the fly only attack the flower stalks.

From this distance it seems that more and more this will be the scenario. For, as new chemicals are marketed their fate will surely follow the same course of those recently excommunicated.

Specific problems associated with the various fruits are dealt with separately under each heading.

PESTS

Ants
An indirect pest insofar that they do no actual damage to plants other than sometimes eroding the soil around the roots. Their mission is in farming aphids sometimes occurring on the roots and moving them from plant to plant. The sight of their activity running along stems is a warning of aphids.

Aphis
Blackfly and greenfly cluster around young terminal growths piercing the tissue and sucking the sap, thereby being a prime vector of viruses. Unchecked, serious damage may result.

Birds
Sparrows, blue tits and bullfinches may from time to time account for some degree of depredation. Bullfinches being particularly destructive on apples and pears while sparrows have a rather catholic taste. First indications are usually a scattering of bud parts underneath the plant mostly at bud burst or a little earlier.

Caterpillars
Itinerant caterpillars of various persuasions feed upon the foliage of many shrubs from time to time. Among which the Leaf Rolling Sawfly and Tortrix Moth larvae banquet unseen in their purpose built hideouts.

Capsid bugs
In appearance like overgrown aphids scurrying away on disturbance They feed on young shoots and fruitlets, especially apples.

Frog hopper
A fairly minor pest yet unwelcome with its delivery of Cuckoo Spit on soft growth early in the season. Another of the sucking fraternity.

Leaf cutter bee
A nuisance rather than a major pest though nevertheless unwelcome as it disfigures flower and particularly foliage. Perfectly engineered semi-circles are scooped from the leaf margins apparently to furnish the walls of the insect's new abode. *(see picture at right)*

Mealy bug
Clusters of white waxy covered bugs, showing little or no movement and adhering on secluded branch forks and sometimes found on nearby objects and wall crevices.

Moles
A serious pest in some districts if attempting to surface near or underneath a newly planted shrub. Standard mole traps are the only answer.

Rabbits, Muntjac and other animals
Attacks from four-legged animals are best prevented by the erection of a stockade, or at the minimum

ringing individual plants with wire netting. Some sprays appear to give protection.

Red spider mite
Microscopic orange spider-like insect mainly found on the undersides of apical leaves and shoots. In heavy infestations leaves take on an ashen appearance with extensive minute webbing slung from branch to branch. Arid dry conditions are usually a precursor to attack.

Sawfly
The plum sawfly skeletonises the leaves, while the apple sawfly eats into the embryonic fruit. The gooseberry sawfly denudes the bushes of leaves overnight while the rose sawfly rolls a leaf around it feeding unseen.

Sucker
Rather like a well developed greenfly quickly dispersing on nearby movement. Feeds mainly on the undersides of leaves.

Thrips
Minute beetles that puncture leaves and flowers causing spotting and silvery streaks resulting in distortion and blind shoots.

Scale
About 3mm (1/8in) in length they resemble a miniature oyster shell adhering limpet-like to stems and the undersides of leathery leaves of shrubs. Often a sooty mould is observed on lower foliage due to their excretions and provides the first indication of their presence.

Vine weevil
A serious pest on the increase. While the larvae feeding on plant roots is often the cause of complete collapse of their hosts the adult, a night worker, chews irregular pieces from leaf margins *(see below left)*. On disturbance they feign death. Their activities are not restricted to vines. Adults are about two thirds the size of a ladybird. The 12mm (1/2in) long grubs assume a horse shoe shape when disturbed *(see below right)*.

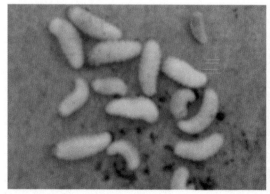

Whitefly
A serious pest under glass but fortunately less so on shrubs outdoors. In severe infections the tiny heart-shaped white flies will be found completely covering the undersides of the foliage. These disperse on disturbing. and retreat into the nymph stage in winter.

DISEASES

Black spot
Badly affects roses with numerous black spots often merging into large patches. Soon causes defoliation, usually worse in a wet season due to the spores being splashed from leaf to leaf. Regular spraying programme essential from April

Canker
Frequently due to waterlogged soils, related to Scab disease which in common with Black Spot is accentuated in wet years. Badly affected trees should be grubbed. Sometimes new replacement growths can be developed in mild attacks.

Coral spot (Nectria cinnabarina) *(see right)*
Aptly named and usually at its height in the winter months. Affects both living and dead tissue including fences from which it will migrate to shrubs. No real cure other than cutting infected wood away, which sometimes appears to work.

Die back
Branches defoliate and become moribund, prevalent on the prunus tribe. Seldom entirely fatal. Probably due to malfunction of the roots.

Downy mildew
Found as orange to whitish small patches mainly on leaf undersides More difficult to control than powdery mildew.

Fireblight (Erwinia amylovora) *(see left)*
Typified by shoots and branches dying back when in leaf and often on the point of flowering. Dead leaves and flowers remain on infected timbers.

Honey Fungus or Boot Lace Fungus. (Armillaria)

A fatal disease which affects a wide range of plants. Symptoms usually develop rapidly from tip die-back, discolouration of the foliage, flower buds failing to open and then general withering of the leaves *(see right)*. Confirmation of the infection can be found by scraping a sliver of bark close to ground level. A white fan-like film or silvery white streaks indicate the presence of the disease *(see below right)*. There is no control other than the immediate removal of the plant and as much of the root base as possible. Left to develop, black boot-lace like growths develop and spread to surrounding subjects and clusters of small brown honey-scented toadstools occur where the infection is established.*(see below left)*. The Royal Horticultural Society publishes an advisory leaflet listing notably resistant genera.

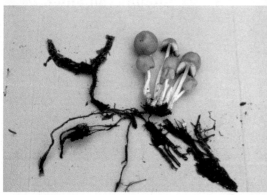

Leaf spots
Numerous forms of leaf spot diseases infect plants from time to time. Any control measures will hopefully ensure that the newly emerging leaves are clear. The existing spots unless treated will remain to further spread the trouble.

Phytophera
Numerous species of this soil-borne disease exhibit the infection by the sudden death of parts of the plant and in severe cases effect a total kill. Control measures difficult if at all.

Powdery Mildew
Gives the appearance of the leaves and young shoots having been dusted with flour. Fortunately easier to control than downy mildew. Extreme dryness at the root often the catalyst.

Rust

Appears as round orange spots usually starting on the undersides of the leaves, and often remaining so with roses, on others subsequently appearing also on the surface.

Scab

Prevalent on many fruits showing as small blackish patches on leaves and later infecting the fruit. Control measures should be put in place early in the season.

Silverleaf fungus

A disease more common to plums, which see.

Wilt

The large-flowered summer clematis are often attacked by this affliction and may be regenerated if the growths are cut hard back to soil level. Initial planting in a tile drain *(see picture right)* is supposed to prevent attack. Many other plants are from time to time so infected due to some physiological disorder for which there is no cure.

Woolly aphis or American Blight (Eriosoma lanigerum). *(see pictures below, left and right)*

A nauseating pest. particularly on apples and to a lesser extent on pears and several ornamentals including pyracantha and cotoneaster horizontalis. The cotton wool like substance is due to the excretions of the aphis. It is most prevalent early in the season and was easily controlled by the standard winter wash treatment with tar oil which has been discontinued.

8
Ornamentals Which Flower During January to March

Abeliophyllum distichum

A somewhat lax hardy growing deciduous shrub to 2m (6ft).

Flowers	Scented, pink-tinged white, borne on bare stems from March to April.
Soil	Ordinary.
Planting Time	Whenever conditions are suitable.
Aspect	South-west.
Pruning	Shorten any lanky shoots after flowering.
Propagation	Hardwood cuttings in cold frame in autumn.
Pests and Diseases	None of note.
Comment	An interesting subject flowering early, though only on well ripened shoots. The foliage often assumes purple shades in autumn.

Acacia
Rapid growing slightly tender evergreen shrubs or small trees to 5m (16ft).

Flowers Bright yellow in scented fluffy clusters from March to May.

Soil	Neutral to acid, well drained.
Planting Time	May.
Aspect	South or west.
Pruning	Shape straggly shoots after flowering.
Propagation	Seed in March in warm propagator. Semi-hardwood cuttings in propagator in June.
Pests and Diseases	Red Spider most likely in arid conditions.

Recommended

armata (Kangaroo Thorn)	A modest evergreen growing to 2m (6ft) with masses of small florets on prickly stems.
dealbata (Silver Wattle)	The familiar "mimosa" of the trade. A strong grower, evergreen, with fern-like foliage. *(see above left)*
pravissima	Strong growing rather lax shrub to about 6m (20ft) with masses of yellow flowers in clusters. Appears to be hardier than other species. *(see above right)*

Comment	All need a very warm corner for surety and should be set well away from the wall to avoid damaging the structure.

Camellia
Hardy evergreen shrub or small tree to about 5m (16ft).

Flowers	Ranging from white to pale yellow, pink and rich red some with colour breaking. Long flowering period.
Soil	Neutral to acid, 6.5ph to 5ph. Enriched with humus.
Planting Time	At most times, avoiding frost and drought.
Aspect	Ideally north-facing with protection from the east.
Pruning	Careful shaping of wayward shoots after flowering.
Propagation	Leaf bud cuttings in heat, early spring. Cuttings in cold frame in early autumn.
Pests and Diseases	Generally trouble free though several problems may arise from time to time including patches of yellow mosaic virus though seemingly not injurious. Cushion scale sometimes attack the undersides of the leaves. Very recently a flower blight has been recorded, attacking their bases and spreading upwards.

Recommended

japonica	Extensive number of cultivars in a distinct range of form.
japonica 'Bob Hope'	Deep crimson, semi-double, compact.
japonica 'Elegans'	Peach-pink, anemone form with bushy habit.
japonica 'Jupiter'	A striking scarlet single with boss of golden stamens. *(see above)*
japonica 'Alba Simplex'	Probably the best white for outdoor use and is a good partner for 'Jupiter' which has a similar flower type. *(see overleaf lower right)*

x *williamsii*	Numerous hybrids equally hardy, and often identified from *C. japonica* in having narrower pointed leaves.
x *williamsii* 'Donation'	Probably the most planted, and rightly so. A semi-double, rich pink, which is a strong grower. *(see above left)*
x *williamsii* 'J C Williams'	A single with soft pink blooms.
x *williamsii* 'St Ewe'	A cup-shaped single with rose pink blooms which flowers over a long period. *(see above upper right)*

Comment   These are much overlooked shrubs offering a distinct ease of culture. Contrary to popular opinion they are very tolerant of dry conditions and will take a much lower degree of acidity than often supposed. White varieties are somewhat chancy due to their petals scorching in windy conditions. Ideally suited for tub cultivation and easily transplanted to the open garden as and when desired. Flower buds are formed in August and September at which time it is important to ensure that they are kept well watered if in a drought regime.

Chaenomeles (Japanese Quince or 'Japonica')
Somewhat straggly hardy deciduous shrubs to about 2m (6ft).

Flowers	Ranging from white, lime to pink and red, open saucer-shaped about the size of a 50 pence piece.
Soil	Ordinary
Planting Time	If bare rooted, November to March. If containerised then whenever conditions are favourable.
Aspect	Any
Pruning	Shaping straggly roots after flowering and again in late summer if needed, following excessive growth.
Propagation	By removal of suckers in autumn.
Pests and Diseases	Seldom troublesome though liable to mildew scab and aphids if in a cloistered position.

Recommended

speciosa	A score or more of cultivars on offer including: -
speciosa 'Apple Blossom'	Pale pink and white.
speciosa 'Geisha Girls'	A striking new introduction. *(see next page bottom)*
speciosa 'Nivalis'	Pure white. *(see above)*
speciosa 'Simonii'	Blood red.
speciosa 'Umbilicata'	Deep salmon-pink.
x *superba*	A similar number of variants, the popular ones include: -
x *superba* 'Crimson and Gold'	Richly coloured with a striking boss of golden stamens.
x *superba* 'Pink Lady'	Clear rose-pink, very early.*(see next page top)*
x *superba* 'Rowallane'	Rich crimson, large flowered.

Comment	A superb plant set anywhere. Shrubs succeeding as trained subjects, free standing bushes or in hedge form. Roundish golden quinces produced in autumn make a fine preserve.

Chimonanthus praecox (Wintersweet)
Fairly vigorous highly scented hardy deciduous shrub to 2m (6ft).

Flowers	Rather insignificant of pale yellow and somewhat cup shaped of a wavy texture. Strongly scented.
Soil	Ordinary well drained.
Planting Time	Container specimens whenever conditions are favourable. Bare rooted from November to March.
Aspect	South or west.
Pruning	Shortly after flowering, reducing the most vigorous shoots.
Propagation	Layering in autumn, seed in cold frame in spring.
Pests and Diseases	Little, if any, of note.
Recommended	
'Grandiflorus'	Deeper yellow flowers stained red.
'Luteus'	Pure yellow flowers produced later than the type.
Comment	The intensely fragrant flowers though rather inconspicuous add a distinct charm to a mild January day. It grows best on a warm wall

Clematis armandii
Slightly tender evergreen twiner to 6m (18ft).

Flowers	Creamy white, very fragrant, borne in clusters from March onwards.
Soil	Ordinary, moist but well drained and humus enriched.
Planting Time	May to July.
Aspect	Sheltered south or west-facing.
Pruning	Shorten excessive shoots after flowering.
Propagation	Internodal cuttings from May to July in a warm propagator, layering September.
Pests and Diseases	Mostly trouble free though leaf scorch sometimes occurs in early spring.
Recommended 'Pink Blossom'	An improved form *(see inserted picture above)* with broader sepals and a pink cast, particularly in bud. Foliage bronzy green.
Comment	The first clematis to flower and in dramatic form *(see main picture above)*. A vigorous grower worth protecting in severe winters. The foliage often becomes untidy after flowering and should be cut back and new growths trained in.

Daphne bholua
A hardy compact evergreen to about 2m (6ft)

Flowers	Pink or white highly fragrant from January to April.
Soil	Light, leafy (with added fine bark, peat or leaf mould).
Planting Time	September or April to May.
Aspect	South or west.
Pruning	Nothing more than an occasional tidy.
Propagation	Layering in autumn.
Pests and Diseases	None of note.
Recommended	
'Alba'	Pure white form with a strong scent.
'Jacqueline Postill'	Has large, purplish pink flowers which are strongly scented and make useful cut flowers.
Comment	A stunning sight when seen in bloom during the first weeks of the year. A fine example adorns the laboratory wall at Wisley. A position most suited to its needs.

Euonymus fortunei
Hardy evergreen shrub.

Flowers	Insignificant, pale green, July.
Soil	Ordinary.
Planting Time	Whenever conditions are favourable.
Aspect	Any, particularly suited to light shade.
Pruning	An occasional light clipping, tipping leaders.
Propagation	Semi-hardwood cuttings in cold frame or layering in autumn.
Pests and Diseases	Mildew if the roots are allowed to become very dry. Caterpillar damage occasionally occurs.
Recommended	
'Coloratus'	Strong growing with rich green leaves which turn crimson purple over winter, returning to green in spring.
'Emerald Gaiety'	Small-leaved bushy plant with green leaves, marginated white, which turn pink in the winter. *(see above left with 'Emerald 'n' Gold')*
'Emerald 'n' Gold'	Similar to 'Emerald Gaiety' but with a gold margin. *(see above bottom right)*
'Silver Pillar'	More upright margins of narrow leaves, white.
'Silver Queen'	The new leaves open attractive creamy-yellow and develop a broad creamy margin. The flowers are more conspicuous and are followed by pinkish capsules in autumn. *(see above top right)*
Comment	A wide selection of indispensable evergreen shrubs ostensibly hummock forming, and rather slow climbing a wall or fence given a modicum of support. Effective throughout the year.

Forsythia suspensa
Vigorous growing hardy deciduous shrub to 5m (16ft)

Flowers	Bright yellow borne en masse.
Soil	Ordinary.
Planting Time	From pots when conditions allow, bare-rooted November to March.
Aspect	Any, though rather wasteful of a south or west site.
Pruning	Immediately after flowering, training in long growths and spurring back laterals.
Propagation	Layering in Autumn or hardwood cuttings in the open ground.
Pests and Diseases	Fasciation sometimes appears, remove as necessary.
Recommended	
'Atrocaulis'	New growth purplish black with lemon yellow flowers.
Comment	Easy and reliable performer if a little rampant with lax growth; of little interest after flowering.
	Ideal subject to support a clematis of modest vigour, such as *C. sieboldii*.

Garrya elliptica
Strong growing evergreen shrubs to 4m (13ft).

Flowers	Minute on long greyish-green catkins. January to March.
Soil	Ordinary.
Planting Time	Whenever conditions are favourable except January and February.
Aspect	Any, especially north-facing.
Pruning	Modest attention to wayward shoots after flowering.
Propagation	Short semi-hard cuttings in cold frame or layering in autumn.
Pests and Diseases	None of note though foliage may burn in severe winters.
Recommended	
'James Roof'	Generally more vigorous than the common form with catkins to about 20cm (8in) in length.
Comment	An outstanding winter flowering subject. Once sited it resents being moved. Some protection may be prudent in cold districts if weather severe. The above subjects are male and are the only forms likely to be offered. The female is rather inconspicuous at flowering time but comes into its own with clusters of purple fruits later. Seldom to be found in garden centres.

Jasminum nudiflorum
Deciduous scandent shrub to 4m (13ft).

Flowers	Canary yellow from December to March.
Soil	Ordinary.
Planting Time	Whenever favourable conditions apply.
Aspect	Any, much favoured for north-facing sites.
Pruning	Immediately after flowering, shortening unnecessary lengthy stems. Will stand hard cutting back.
Propagation	Layering tips of the current season's growth.
Pests and Diseases	None of note.
Recommended 'Aureum'	Leaves heavily splashed yellow.
Comment	An indispensable shrub to brighten the winter scene. Flowers likely to suffer in hard frost but quickly replaced when conditions improve.

Kerria japonica
A hardy stiffish deciduous shrub to 2m (6ft).

Flowers	Butter yellow, the size of a 10p coin, from February onwards.
Soil	Ordinary.
Planting Time	Whenever suitable conditions allow.
Aspect	Any, but a front runner for the north.
Pruning	Removal of flowered stems in May and June.
Propagation	By division November to March.
Pests and Diseases	Seemingly free.

Recommended

'Pleniflora'   Familiar fully double form. *(see above)*

'Variegata'   A pretty cream variegated form, less stiff in growth.

Comment   A strong feature of the Kerrias is their bright green stems especially when kept well pruned, these being most conspicuous in winter. They often flower for many weeks given a prime lightly shaded position, even commencing in autumn.

Abutilon
Slightly tender evergreen to about 2m (6ft).

Flowers	Bell-shaped, orange and blue to yellow and white, from May to December.
Soil	Ordinary, well drained.
Planting Time	Late April and May.
Aspect	South or west.
Pruning	Cut weak laterals hard back, after securing leaders, at end of April.
Propagation	Softwood cuttings anytime in a heated propagator.
Pests and Diseases	Aphids troublesome, usually occurring only on flower stalks.

Recommended

'Kentish Belle'	A remarkably lax growing shrub for a warm position, flowering over many months. *(see above right)*
megapotamicum	Of similar habit to 'Kentish Belle' though slightly more tender and with smaller flowers about the size of a 10p coin.
megapotamicum 'Variegatum'	As above, with the addition of bright yellow blotching on the narrow, long, triangular-pointed foliage. *(see above lower left)*
vitifolium	Pale to deep mauve flowers the size of a coffee cup saucer. *(see upper left)*
vitifolium 'Album'	As above but with pure white flowers. *(see above lower right)*
vitifolium 'Suntense'	Reckoned to be an improvement on the common variety.

Comment	Advisable to protect the lower 45cm (18in) from severe frost with straw, bracken or other materials. Regeneration may then be assured should the winter prove particularly hard. Mostly, problems are few. Continuity of flower is a considerable attribute. I recall seeing the flowers of 'Kentish Belle' when slightly expanded used as 'Water Lilies' in finger bowls. In the very top drawer of wall shrubs.

Actinidia
Hardy deciduous twining shrubs.

Flowers	Slightly fragrant, buff yellow, from May onwards.
Soil	Ordinary.
Planting Time	May.
Aspect	South or west.
Pruning	Shorten vigorous growths in spring to foster development of lateral spurs.
Propagation	Seed in cold frame in spring, layering in autumn.
Pests and Diseases	Little if any problem as a rule.

Recommended

chinensis Chinese Gooseberry or Kiwi Fruit - *(see Fruit section, page 198)*

kolomitka (see above) Less vigorous than the above but noted for its striking leaf colour. The leaves are up to 15cm (6in) and ranging in green at the stalk end to pure white and ending in pink. Some leaves are almost devoid of green, but eventually as summer proceeds, the colour returns.

Comment Young plants often take several years to give of their best. Young growth subject to late spring frost damage. A west wall is generally best.

Akebia

Vigorous semi-evergreen hardy twiner.

Flowers	Fragrant male and female, purple, borne on drooping sprays in April.
Soil	Well-drained humus-rich.
Planting Time	May.
Aspect	South or west.
Pruning	Shorten straggly shoots after flowering.
Propagation	Semi-hardwood cuttings in a warm propagator, layering in autumn.
Pests and Diseases	Mainly trouble free, though mildew may occur in a dry season.
Recommended	
quinata	Compound five-fingered leaves, maroon sausage-shaped fruits 5-10cm (2-4in) long. *(see.picture above)*
Comment	A strong grower which is ideal cascading over a wall. A successful crop of fruits is dependent upon a frost free spring and warm summer.

Asteranthera ovata
A rather tender, lax trailing evergreen with small ovate leaves.

Flowers	Rich blood red with conspicuous white throat, tubular, from May onwards.
Soil	Leafy, moist.
Planting Time	May.
Aspect	Lightly shaded woodland or north wall.
Pruning	None necessary.
Propagation	By semi-hardwood cuttings in a warm propagator at most times, or by seed in heat.
Pests and Diseases	None of note.
Comment	A luxuriously attractive scrambling evergreen for favoured gardens in the south or west including Scotland. It has survived several winters in East Anglia and will climb a damp north-facing wall.

Azara
Slightly tender evergreen shrub to 3m (10ft).

Flowers	Golden with small globular heads in May.
Soil	Ordinary.
Planting Time	April, May.
Aspect	South, west, or east in sheltered gardens.
Pruning	No detailed, slight shaping as desired after flowering.
Propagation	Semi-hard cuttings in a warm propagator in summer.
Pests and Diseases	Generally free.
Recommended	
dentata	Similar to *serrata*
microphylla	Has fern-like foliage with myriads of tiny mimosa like flowers on the undersides of its branches.
serrata	*(see picture above)*
Comment	Exceptionally floriferous, *microphylla* makes a handsome foliage contribution all year round.

Brugmansia suaveolens (Datura or Angel's Trumpets)
A strong growing tender deciduous shrub to 2m (6ft).

Flowers	Large trumpet-shaped with flared mouth from April onwards.
Soil	Ordinary, well drained.
Planting Time	May.
Aspect	South-west.
Pruning	As growth commences in March.
Propagation	By seed sown in a warm propagator or semi-hardwood shoots during summer
Pests and Diseases	Both White Fly and Red Spider likely to prove troublesome.
Recommended	
sanguinea	Handsome orange-shaded trumpets *(see above right)*
suaveolens	Trumpets pure white. *(see above left)*
Comment	Striking shrubs only suited to outdoor cultivation in the extreme south-west, otherwise good patio subjects in a container. The base of the plant should be protected in winter.

Carpenteria californica (Tree Anemone)
Modest bushy, slightly tender, evergreen growing to about 3m (10ft).

Flowers	Pure white with prominent boss of golden anthers in June.
Soil	Ordinary well drained.
Planting Time	April and May.
Aspect	South or west.
Pruning	Removal of spent flower stems and occasional light shaping.
Propagation	Semi-hardwood cuttings in cold frame in August.
Pests and Diseases	Conspicuous by their absence.
Comment	An exquisitely beautiful and much coveted wall shrub of modest growth. Some light protection advisable in severe winters especially in northern districts.

Ceanothus (Californian Lilac)

A large group of hardy evergreen and some deciduous subjects to about 5m (16ft).

Flowers	Borne in tight, deep blue to white trusses, from May onwards.
Soil	Ordinary, well drained.
Planting Time	April to May or September.
Aspect	South or west.
Pruning	Early flowering varieties immediately after the flowers have faded, though seldom requiring much attention.
Propagation	Softwood cuttings mid-summer in a warm propagator. Semi-hardwood in cold frame in September.
Pests and Diseases	Almost trouble free.

Recommended

arboreus 'Trewithian Blue'	Strong growing, almost tree-like, with bright blue flowers, often continuously, slightly fragrant.
'Burkwoodii'	Medium shrub with dark blue flowers in mid-summer.
'Concha'	Clusters of tightly packed deep blue flowers.
dentatus	Of modest habit, but producing masses of early, powder-blue flowers.
impressus	A strong grower with heavily indented venation, reckoned to be one of the hardiest for general planting. *(see above)*
'Puget Blue'	Of modest habit but with deep blue flowers from spring onwards.
'Snow Flurries'	A medium grower with pure white flowers.
thyrsiflorus	A very hardy strong grower with early bright blue flowers.
x *veitchianus*	Early and very hardy with glossy leaves and deep blue flowers.

Comment	Rank amongst our most reliable performers in all but the very coldest part of the land. Tolerant of very dry conditions. Unfortunately not noted for longevity and does not break from bare wood very well. See later for the later-flowering deciduous varieties.

Choisya ternata (Mexican Orange Blossom)
A hardy evergreen shrub with attractive foliage to 2m (6ft).

Flowers	White in scented clusters in May, and often again in August *(see lower picture)*.
Soil	Ordinary, well drained.
Planting Time	Whenever favourable conditions apply.
Aspect	North, south and west.
Pruning	Shaping up after initial flowering with any heavy work carried out in late March.
Propagation	Semi-hardwood cuttings in warm propagator in summer. Firm cuttings in cold frame in autumn.
Pests and Diseases	None of note.
Recommended	
'Aztec Pearl'	The foliage is further divided into almost fern-like appearance *(see upper left)*.
'Sundance'	Develops brilliant gold foliage only when planted in full sun *(see upper right)*.
'Goldfinger'	A golden form of 'Aztec Pearl'.
Comment	All are of rapid growth, and although unfortunately subject to damage in heavy snow, they regenerate well.

Clematis
Hardy deciduous climbers assisted by clasping leaf stems.

Flowers	From April onwards, ranging from white through blue, yellow and red. Some bell or vase shaped, others flattish.
Soil	Well drained yet nicely moist.
Planting Time	May or early September.
Aspect	Most positions suitable though north slightly less so.
Pruning	The early ones may be hard pruned after flowering for containment, or left to luxuriate as desired. The mid-summer large hybrids require little detailed pruning save lightly trimming wayward stems. Overgrown ones may be hard pruned in March, resulting in renewed growth but delaying the flowering period substantially.
Propagation	Layering in autumn or by soft and semi-hardwood internodal cuttings in a warm propagator from May to July.
Pests and Diseases	Generally free though affected by aphids and mildew on occasion. Clematis wilt among the hybrids is more prevalent in some areas than others.

Recommended

alpina	A modest slender climber with nodding bell-shaped flowers borne on long stalks in May.
alpina 'Frances Rivis'	Larger flowers and stronger growing than the type. *(see above left)*
alpina 'Ruby'	Flowers rosy-red.
alpina var. *sibirica*	Flowers creamy white.
x *durandii*	Dark blue flowers up to 10cm (4in) diameter with bright cluster of yellow stamens from late June onwards.
macropetala	Vigorous with a prolific crop of nodding bell-shaped flowers followed by fluffy seed heads which persist for some weeks. *(see above right)*
macropetala 'Markhamii'	Also known as 'Markham's Pink', is a pretty lavender pink form flowering all April and May with fluffy seed heads. There are also several white forms.

montana (The Mountain Clematis)	The pure white flowers are nicely scented. All the following selections are extremely vigorous and need ample room for the best effect. *(see upper left with C. montana rubens)*
montana 'Elizabeth'	Pale pink flowers
montana 'Freda'	Dark pink with deeper edges.
montana 'Grandiflora'	The purest white form.
montana 'Rubens'	Rich pink, with a sheen of purple on the foliage. The flowers are smaller than the other types.
montana 'Tetrarose'	Bronze leaves with large rosy-lilac flowers in mid-May.
orientalis	A vigorous twining shrub with yellow nodding flowers of a waxy texture. Masses of fluffy seed heads follow. Grows to about 5m (16ft).
orientalis 'Orange Peel'	Has thicker sepals than *orientalis*.
florida var. *bicolor* ('Sieboldii')	*(see above upper right)* Creamy white flowers with a large boss of petaloid stamens of a rich dark blue. An outstanding and unusual form, of modest growth.
tangutica	*(see above lower left)* Similar to orientalis but slightly taller and less graceful, with lantern-like yellow flowers in May, followed by 'Old mans beard' seed heads from July onwards.*(see above lower right)*

Large-flowered mid-season hybrids

'Barbara Jackman' Soft petunia-mauve with crimson bars and cream stamens. *(see above lower right)*

'Comtesse de Bouchard' Rich deep pink with flowers slightly smaller than average, over a long period from June onwards. *(see above lower left)*

'Ernest Markham' Glowing petunia-red and flowering over a long period.

'Gipsy Queen' Impressive violet-purple flowers over a long period.

'Nelly Moser' Pale mauve-pink with crimson central bars from May to June. Abundant flowers but tending to fade in full sun. *(see above upper left)*

'Niobe' Dramatic rich deep ruby red, the darkest to date, with contrasting golden stamens. *(see above upper right)*

'Prince Charles' Lilac-blue smallish flowers with green stamens from June onwards. *(see next page top)*

'Princess Diana' An arresting variety, appropriately named *(see next page bottom)*

Comment Most of the modern hybrids are of easy cultivation.

Cytisus battandieri (Moroccan Broom)

Strong growing semi-evergreen hardy shrub to 4m (13ft) from June onwards.

Flowers	Bright yellow cone-shaped from June with a pineapple appearance, the scent of which it curiously resembles.
Soil	Ordinary, light.
Planting Time	Whenever conditions are favourable.
Aspect	South or west.
Pruning	Removal of spent flowered shoots, training in strong growths fan-wise.
Propagation	Seed sown outdoors in March or April.
Pests and Diseases	Fortunately nothing of note.
Comment	An unusual and striking shrub with attractive silky foliage giving an overall silver sheen. Best grown against a wall north of the Midlands. In the South it makes a fine free standing shrub of vigorous growth. Attention needs to be paid for unwanted suckers, as it is often grafted onto Laburnum.

Dendromecon rigida (Tree Poppy)
Large evergreen hardy shrub with silvery pointed leaves.

Flowers	Poppy-like fragrant yellow flowers from May onwards throughout the summer.
Soil	Well drained with added rubble.
Planting Time	April to May.
Aspect	South or west.
Pruning	Removal of spent shoots in April.
Propagation	Semi-hardwood cuttings in a warm propagator in July.
Pests and Diseases	None of note.
Comment	Essentially a subject for a warm wall and requiring protection in severe weather. Makes an impressive plant.

Desfontania spinosa

A slightly tender evergreen shrub with distinctive holly-like leaves to about 2m (6ft).

Flowers	Arresting scarlet and yellow trumpets 5cm (2in) long in June.
Soil	Neutral to slightly acid. Humus rich.
Planting Time	April to May.
Aspect	South or west with light shading.
Pruning	Removal of spent flower shoots in spring.
Propagation	Semi-hardwood cuttings in a warm propagator in spring.
Pests and Diseases	None of note.
Comment	A very striking and unusual subject not entirely hardy though over-wintering satisfactorily in East Anglia. Some protection advisable in severe weather away from the west coasts. It makes a close-growing compact bush.

Dicentra scandens

Hardy herbaceous perennial climbing by means of tendrils to 1.5m (5ft).

Flowers	Bright yellow from April onwards in the style of a Dutchman's breeches.
Soil	Light rich.
Planting Time	April
Aspect	South, east or west, sheltered.
Pruning	Removal of old stems at ground level in March.
Propagation	Division of roots in March. Seed in warm propagator or cold frame in summer.
Pests and Diseases	Generally none, though aphids may prove troublesome.
Comment	A most unusual subject of a very popular genus which is worth training through a sparsely growing shrub.

Eccremocarpus scaber

Hardy semi-evergreen which climbs rapidly by means of tendrils.

Flowers	Tube-like, freely produced, yellow, orange or crimson.
Soil	Ordinary, light.
Planting Time	April to May.
Aspect	South, east or west.
Pruning	May be hard cut back in April or merely having the older growths and inflated seed heads removed.
Propagation	By seed under glass March to April. Cuttings in warm propagator from May onwards.
Pests and Diseases	Apparently none.
Comment	Makes a very presentable effort on its own and a useful additive for scrambling through an evergreen such as Ceanothus. Has pretty fern-like foliage and seeds prolifically in sandy soils.

Ercilla volubilis
Hardy evergreen shrub climbing by aerial roots to 4m (14ft).

Flowers	Pinkish in dense spikes in April.
Soil	Ordinary light.
Planting Time	September or April.
Aspect	South and west.
Pruning	Shorten wayward shoots after flowering.
Propagation	By hardwood cuttings or layering in autumn.
Pests and Diseases	Generally free.
Comment	Self supporting against a wall and shade tolerant and useful for blanket cover. The tight, grape-like, flower trusses are of little appeal.

Eriobotrya japonica (Loquat)

Slightly tender evergreen shrub growing to 2m (6ft) with large leathery leaves.

Flowers	Hawthorn like and scented, in white corymbs, borne in June only in hot summers. Yellow edible fruits.
Soil	Ordinary.
Planting Time	April to May.
Aspect	South or west.
Pruning	Tie in main rods and shorten weak shoots in April.
Propagation	Semi-hardwood cuttings in cold frame in autumn. Seed in cold frame in spring or autumn.
Pests and Diseases	Almost free.
Comment	An impressive plant for a large wall requiring some protection in all but the most favoured southerly gardens. Worth growing solely for its impressive foliage.

Hebe
Slightly tender evergreen lowly shrubs.

Flowers	Tapering racemes, white to red or blue, April onwards, mostly from mid-summer.
Soil	Ordinary, well drained.
Planting Time	April and May.
Aspect	South or west.
Pruning	Early ones, immediately after flowering, removing spent growths. Later ones, prune into shape the following spring.
Propagation	By softwood cuttings in warm propagator April to July.
Pests and Diseases	Leaf spot often troublesome on some, aphids also.
Recommended	
'Great Orme'	Flowering from June to August and perhaps the hardiest of those with a reddish colour, it grows to a height of 1.5m (4.5ft).
hulkeana	Reckoned to be the most striking Hebe, 1m (3ft) tall, with light blue flowers in long tapering branched trusses. *(see above)*
'La Seduisante'	Bright crimson flowers of typical, though shortened form, borne over a long period from mid-summer and in very favoured positions all through the year. Grows 1.5m (4.5ft) tall.
Comment	Mostly native to the antipodes and suffer badly in very severe winters. Will regenerate from hard pruning when growth restarts, which may be as late as June.

Hydrangea petiolaris (Climbing Hydrangea)
Hardy, strong growing, self clinging deciduous climber.

Flowers	Handsome white corymbs of lace-cap form in June and July.
Soil	Rich, ordinary texture.
Planting Time	Whenever suitable conditions apply.
Aspect	North, west and east.
Pruning	Removal of flowered laterals in spring.
Propagation	Layering in autumn, semi-hardwood cuttings from May to July in warm propagator.
Pests and Diseases	Little if any, aphids sometimes on young tips.
Comment	In the forefront of subjects to furnish a north-facing aspect. Often very slow to start serious growing. While aerial roots support young growth these soon die back so needing occasional added support. An outstanding example may be found at Felbrigg Hall, Norfolk *(see above left)*.

Leptospermum
Rather tender evergreen shrub to 2m (6ft).

Flowers	White to crimson, mostly small about the size of a five pence piece from June on.
Soil	Well drained, light.
Planting Time	May.
Aspect	South to west, well sheltered.
Pruning	Light, as desired, in spring.
Propagation	Short firm cuttings in cold frame in autumn.
Pests and Diseases	Generally free.

Recommended

lanigerum   Flowers white with silvery foliage turning bronze in autumn. Hardier than most.

scoparium   The principal species with numerous hybrids including double-flowered and dwarf forms. *(see above, left and right)*

Comment   Almost entirely the prerogative of gardens in the south west. Much cosseting needed further north though worth a chance in a well sheltered environment.

Lomatia ferruginia
Tender evergreen shrub to 4m (13ft).

Flowers	Reddish to white in June
Soil	Ordinary well drained.
Planting Time	May to June.
Aspect	South or west.
Pruning	Shaping as necessary after flowering.
Propagation	Semi-hardwood cuttings in a warm propagator from June onwards.
Pests and Diseases	None of note.
Comment	Striking fern-like foliage. Hardy in the extreme south-west, requires cosseting elsewhere.

Lonicera
Hardy deciduous or evergreen twiners.

Flowers	Narrow tube-like in clusters, mostly scented, from May onwards.
Soil	Well prepared.
Planting Time	Spring or early autumn.
Aspect	Any.
Pruning	Trim off excessive growths in March and cut hard back if dealing with old plants.
Propagation	Layering in autumn, semi-hardwood cuttings in warm propagator in summer. Hardwood cuttings in cold frame.
Pests and Diseases	Most are subject to the attention of aphids in their early stages of growth. Mildew on occasions.

Recommended

x *americana*	Vigorous with highly scented flowers, white deepening to yellow.
x *brownii*	(Scarlet Trumpet Honeysuckle) Semi-evergreen with scentless, fairly continuous orange red flowers.
x *brownii* 'Dropmore Scarlet'	An improved form with brighter red flowers. *(see above right)*
x *heckrottii* 'Gold Flame'	Fragrant yellow flowers with a purple flush.
japonica 'Aureoreticulata'	Scented rather insignificant white flowers. Small golden leaves highlighted by striking venation. Best in full sun. *(see above left)*
'Halliana'	Vigorous scrambling evergreen continuously flowering with strongly scented pale yellow to white flowers. *(see next page lower left)*
'Hall's Prolific'	A selected more floriferous form of the above.
var. *repens*	Leaves and shoots tinged purple, flowers highly fragrant.
periclymenum (Woodbine)	The native honeysuckle with flowers white turning yellowish followed by glistening red berries in autumn.

'Belgica'	(Early Dutch Honeysuckle) Bears very strongly scented flowers, rosy-red on the outside, yellow inside in May.
'Graham Thomas'	A stronger growing form with flowers cream, deepening to yellow.
'Harlequin'	Similar flowers to 'Belgica' but with foliage blotched pink and cream.
periclymenum 'Serotina'	(Late Dutch Honeysuckle) As highly scented as 'Belgica' but with much deeper coloured flowers in June *(see above upper left)*.
similis	Striking individual flowers in June, white to primrose and scented. *(see above lower right)*
x *tellmaniana*	Distinctive large leaved oval foliage with golden-yellow flowers flushed red in the bud in June *(see above upper right)*.
tragophylla	A striking form with some of the largest foliage and flowers of the genus. Bright golden-yellow flowers in June and red berries in autumn.

Comment	In the forefront of twining shrubs, all of easy culture, suited to all aspects with a slant towards the more shaded spots. Most are heavily perfumed, others make up for the lack of it with striking flowers.

Maurandia scandens
Rampant rather tender evergreen slender climber.

Flowers	Tubelike, whitish with lilac flanged mouth, borne singly in June on wands.
Soil	Light, well drained.
Planting Time	May.
Aspect	Sheltered south-west.
Pruning	Reduction of excessive growths in spring. Regenerates well from the base.
Propagation	By seed in warm propagator, softwood cuttings likewise.
Pests and Diseases	White Fly may prove troublesome.
Comment	One of the daintiest of climbing plants, ideally left to scramble through some host shrub. Has a herbaceous tendency and is reasonably hardy, though best given winter protection away from southern gardens. Cutting hard back to soil level and covering with a cloche may prove a useful ploy.

Mimulus aurantiacus (The Shrubby Musk)
Slightly tender evergreen shrub to 1.2m(4ft).

Flowers	Orange, flared-trumpet shape from May onwards to autumn
Soil	Ordinary.
Planting Time	May.
Aspect	South-west.
Pruning	Shortening laterals severely in April to overcome any waywardness.
Propagation	By softwood cuttings in warm propagator at most times of the year.Quick to root.
Pests and Diseases	Singularly free.
Recommended	
glutinosus	The familiar orange-yellow form. *(see above)*
'Puniceus'	Flowers crimson, with foliage slightly smaller and darker green than the type.
Comment	A most floriferous and dainty shrub flowering incessantly but with stems and flowers tacky. A useful infiller against a warm wall. Protect the base in winter. Tacky stems and foliage make taking cuttings a messy business.

Olearia macrodonta (New Zealand Holly)
A strong growing hardy evergreen shrub to about 3m (10ft).

Flowers	Daisy-like, white, in clusters freely borne in May and June.
Soil	Ordinary well drained.
Planting Time	April to May.
Aspect	South-west.
Pruning	Removal of spent flower heads after flowering.
Propagation	By semi-hardwood cuttings in a warm propagator during summer.
Pests and Diseases	None of note.
Recommended	
macrodonta	A strong grower with holly-like leaves. *(see above left)*
macrodonta 'Minor'	Much smaller in all its parts.
scillionensis	Exceptional free flowering silver-foliaged shrub to 1m (3ft) or slightly more in May. *(see above right)*
Comment	*O. macrodonta* is hardy in most gardens though some care needed in its placement in the north. *O. scillionensis* is less hardy and needs protection in cold areas. Both species are rapid in growth and front rank plants. Will stand cutting back hard in April.

Osmanthus x burkwoodii (Fragrant Olive)

A robust hardy evergreen shrub to 2m (6ft).

Flowers	Small, white and very fragrant in April.
Soil	Ordinary.
Planting Time	Whenever conditions permit.
Aspect	Any, and a good choice for a north-facing position.
Pruning	Light trimming if desired after flowering. Responds to formal hedging.
Propagation	Ripened short shoots in cold frame in autumn.
Pests and Diseases	None of note.

Recommended

x *burkwoodii*	*(see above left and upper right)*
delavayii	Slightly larger with numerous highly scented flowers. *(see above lower right)*
heteropyllus	Holly-like shrub with white, scented, flowers in October. Dense format and ideal for hedges but slightly less hardy.
'Variegatus'	Leaves bordered creamy white.
Comment	These are tough, go-anywhere, scented shrubs. Sometimes rather slow to establish

Paeonia lutea *(Tree Peony)*
A hardy deciduous shrub to 2m (6ft).

Flowers	Golden cups in May.
Soil	Rich, well worked.
Planting Time	May.
Aspect	Sheltered against a warm wall in the south-west.
Pruning	None required.
Propagation	By suckers or layering in autumn, or seed in a cold frame.
Pests and Diseases	None of note.

Recommended
lutea — An impressive shrub when in full bloom.
var. *ludlowii* 'Sherriff's Variety' — A superior form with larger flowers. (see above)

Comment — While intrinsically fully hardy, growth commences early and so is liable to frost damage. Worth growing for its ornamental foliage alone. Produces heavy crops of seed on occasions.

Phlomis fruticosa (Jerualem Sage)
A small hardy evergreen shrub

Flowers	Rich golden-yellow whorls on long stems in June.
Soil	Ordinary, well drained.
Planting Time	April to September.
Aspect	Any except north.
Pruning	Removal of the lengthy spent flower stems, trimming as required in April.
Propagation	Ripened shoots in cold frame in autumn.
Pests and Diseases	None of note.
Comment	A most invaluable plant for a hot sunny position, the silky foliage complementing other colours throughout the year. Though low growing it may be easily trained up a wall or fence and is fully hardy in most areas.

Pieris

Hardy evergreen close growing shrubs with striking red young foliage that gradually turns to green.

Flowers	Trusses of pink buds are formed in September and held tight until spring. Florets, white to pink, lily of the valley-like.
Soil	Ericaceous ph 5 - 6.5.
Planting Time	September to October or April to May.
Aspect	North or shaded west.
Pruning	Generally not required but will stand severe cutting back.
Propagation	Layering in autumn.
Pests and Diseases	None of note.

Recommended

'Firecrest'	A large shrub with deeply veined broad leaves.
'Flaming Silver'	Has bright red new leaves which soon develop attractive silver markings.
'Forest Flame'	One of the hardiest with brilliant young growths. *(see above right)*
'Wakehurst'	A selection with shorter broad leaves.
japonica (Valley Valentine)	Has large clusters of drooping whitish flowers but is less vigorous than all the above. *(see above left)*
'Variegata'	A conspicuously variegated, but slower growing form.

Comment	All have bright red young leaves vulnerable to both frost and, in the second flush which often appears, to hot sun. A north-facing aspect with light overhead shading is most suitable. They also make good tub plants.

Piptanthus nepalensis (Evergreen Laburnum)
Hardy semi-evergreen to 3m (14ft) of open habit with trifoliate leaves.

Flowers	Bright yellow erect, laburnum-like, in May.
Soil	Ordinary.
Planting Time	April to May.
Aspect	South to west.
Pruning	Removal of flowered shoots.
Propagation	Layering in autumn, semi-hardwood cuttings in cold frame in autumn. Seed in spring under glass.
Pests and Diseases	Nothing of note.
Comment	An attractive and unusual shrub, quick in growth, with crops of bean-like seed pods in favourable seasons. Ideal for a hot situation.

Prostanthera rotundifolia (Mint Bush)
A slightly tender evergreen aromatic shrub to 2m (6ft).

Flowers	Lilac, borne en masse in April
Soil	Light ordinary.
Planting Time	May.
Aspect	South to west.
Pruning	Shortening side-shoots immediately after flowering.
Propagation	Softwood cuttings in warm propagator in summer. Rooting may take a long time.
Pests and Diseases	Nothing of note.
Comment	This charming plant is a winner given a cosy corner over most of the country. Hardy in the south-west, also surviving well in East Anglia in mild winters.

Rhaphithamnus spinosus
A slightly tender bushy evergreen shrub to 2m (6ft).

Flowers	Pale blue in May.
Soil	Light ordinary.
Planting Time	May.
Aspect	South to west, sheltered.
Pruning	Shortening side-shoots as required to maintain shape after flowering.
Propagation	Semi-hardwood cuttings in warm propagator in summer.
Pests and Diseases	Nothing of note.
Comment	An unusual and fascinating wall shrub having leaves equipped with needle-like spines, proving hardy in eastern regions. Flowers tend to be slightly hidden by the foliage.

Ribes speciosum (Fuchsia Flowered Gooseberry)
Hardy deciduous open growing shrub with bristly stems to 1.5m (5ft).

Flowers	Rich red with a strong resemblance to a fuchsia, though narrower and of one hue, in May.
Soil	Ordinary.
Planting Time	Whenever conditions are favourable.
Aspect	South east or west.
Pruning	Train in main stems in autumn and spur-prune laterals.
Propagation	Hardwood cuttings in cold frame in autumn or in a sheltered spot outdoors.
Pests and Diseases	May be affected by gooseberry sawfly caterpillar or that of the Magpie moth. Gooseberry mildew also likely.
Comment	A pretty and distinctive easily trained shrub. A fine example may be seen on the wall outside one of the gents' toilets at Wisley.

Robinia hispida 'Rosea' (Rose Acacia)
Hardy deciduous bush to about 2m (6ft) with bristly stems.

Flowers	Pea-like in pendent racemes of a deep rose colour in May to June.
Soil	Ordinary.
Planting Time	Whenever conditions are suitable.
Aspect	South or west.
Pruning	Removal of flowered stems nearly to their base in autumn.
Propagation	By suckers removed in late autumn.
Pests and Diseases	Little of note though a possibilty of Red Spider.
Comment	A pretty subject with the appearance of a wisteria. Short flowering period often followed by bean-like seed pods. Wandering suckers sometimes can be a nuisance.

Rosa
A large group of hardy deciduous and partly evergreen shrubs.

Flowers	Ranging from deepest red through yellow to purest white in single, semi-double and fully double forms. Many are highly perfumed.
Soil	Most will give a good return, though usually a better result will be achieved from those that are full bodied and deep. Suited to heavy clays.
Planting Time	Bare root specimens from October to March, though ideally not later than Christmas. Container grown at any favourable time.
Aspect	South, east or west. A few will tolerate a north position.
Pruning	After flowering in late autumn. Most ramblers having some of the previous year's stems removed and replaced by the current year's. The ends are shortened as required or in some cases allowed almost free rein. Climbers require to have their main limbs retained save for the occasional removal of an ancient growth.The extension growths are shortened slightly and the side growths trimmed back close to their points of origin. Train as the ribs of a fan with the outward growths as low as practicable.
Propagation	All forms by hardwood cuttings in a sheltered corner of the open ground in September. Ramblers by layering in autumn.
Pests and Diseases	Mildew and Black Spot, along with the more recent incidence of Rust, can be troublesome. Aphids from time to time and Leaf Galls though less serious than the former.

Recommended

Climbing forms - selected list.

banksiae 'Alba Plena'	Fragrant, double white rosettes
banksiae 'Lutea'	(Yellow Banksian Rose) A strong grower for a favourable warm wall with small double rich-yellow scented rosettes. Early flowering and requiring little more than an occasional trim. *(see above left)*
'Bantry Bay'	A strong stiff grower with clusters of bright pink flowers all summer.
'Compassion'	Repeat flowering, with large, fragrant pinkish orange hybrid tea-like flowers.
'Dublin Bay'	Blood red, lightly scented flowers over a short period. *(see page 86 bottom)*
'Etoile de Hollande'	Deep red sweetly scented flowers.
'Gloire de Dijon'	An old fashioned double with strongly scented buff to apricot flowers. Suitable for a north-facing wall.
'Golden Showers'	An abundance of large rich golden flowers and attractive dark green foliage. Suitable for a north wall. *(see page 88 upper left)*
'Guinee'	One of the darkest roses with recurrent scented flowers.
'Iceberg'	Carries the purest white lightly flushed pink flowers, which are often double. Sweetly scented and continuously flowering from May to December. Very disease resistant. *(see page 86 top)*
'Maigold'	Aptly named, early to flower with semi-double scented blooms. Recurrent, almost entirely disease free and suitable for a north-facing wall or fence. *(see previous page)*
'Maigold Improved'	A new sport from 'Maigold'. Rich red buds opening a shade lighter. Most notable early in the season. *(see above right)*

'Mermaid'	Large saucer shaped bright yellow flowers with a striking boss of golden stamens. Continues to flower, though sparsely, from June onwards. Requires the light pruning of straggly shoots and dead heads. *(see page 88 bottom)*
'Pink Perpetue'	*(see page 88 upper right)*
'Schoolgirl'	A fragrant apricot hybrid tea-type with attractive shiny foliage.
'Zephirine Drouhin'	Produces very fragrant recurring rose-pink flowers and is blessed with a complete lack of thorns.

Ramblers

'Alberic Barbier'	Creamy white scented flowers produced early in the season.
'Albertine'	Bears salmon-pink scented flowers early in the season, though only for a short flowering period.
'Emily Grey'	Very pretty golden yellow buds opening to near white with rich green foliage which persists almost all year round. It requires light pruning only.
'Kiftsgate'	Reckoned to be the most vigorous rose in the book with cascades of single white, scented, flowers in panicles from early July. *(see above right)*
'Paul's Scarlet'	Bright scarlet double flowers freely borne. *(see above left)*
'The New Dawn'	Light shell-pink double flowers produced all season.
'Wedding Day'	A vigorous rambler bearing masses of small creamy-white fragrant flowers from July.

| *Comment* | Roses are everyone's favourite and deserve a place on any wall or fence along with the numerous other suitable subjects. The few that tolerate a north position do so under duress, such is their love of sun. |

Rosmarinus officinalis (Common Rosemary)
Hardy evergreen shrub to 2m (6ft).

Flowers	Small rich blue, pea sized, in April to May.
Soil	Ordinary well drained.
Planting Time	In all favourable conditions.
Aspect	South, east or west.
Pruning	As desired immediately after flowering.
Propagation	Semi-hardwood cuttings in cold frame in autumn or warm propagator in summer.
Pests and Diseases	Red Spider could prove troublesome on a hot wall.
Recommended	
'Miss Jessop' AGM	A close growing, fairly columnar form. *(see above)*
Comment	Valued for the richness of its flowers against the greyish foliage, scented and a useful in-filler among other wall shrubs.

Senna corymbosa (Cassia corymbosa)
Rather tender evergreen shrub to 2m (6ft).

Flowers	Butter-yellow in terminal clusters in June.
Soil	Ordinary, well drained.
Planting Time	May.
Aspect	South-west.
Pruning	Trimming for a shapely specimen in March.
Propagation	By seed or hardwood cuttings in warm propagator in March.
Pests and Diseases	Liable to attack by Red Spider in arid conditions.
Comment	A striking shrub usually of greenhouse culture though likely to suceed given a warm well-sheltered niche in southern regions.

Sophora

Slightly tender strong growing upright shrubs, evergreen with small leaflets.

Flowers	Yellow, tubular, pea shaped and in clusters in May.
Soil	Ordinary, well drained.
Planting Time	April to May.
Aspect	South or west, sheltered.
Pruning	Removal of spent flower heads in April.
Propagation	By seed in warm propagator in spring. Semi-hardwood cuttings in cold frame in autumn.
Pests and Diseases	Liable to attack by Red Spider.
Recommended	
microphylla	Early growth, pendent, with tiny leaflets on wiry stems. *(see above left)*
tetraptera	A fairly lax shrub with drooping branchlets, larger flowers and unusual winged seed pods. *(see above right)*
Comment	Candidates for a very warm niche in all but the most favourable of gardens. A superb specimen of *tetraptera* exists on Mersea Island, Essex, fronting the estuary. Both very slow from seed.

Stauntonia hexaphylla

Strong growing, if slightly tender, evergreen twining climber with leathery leaves to 6m (20ft).

Flowers	White, tinged purple, and fragrant in April.
Soil	Light ordinary, deep.
Planting Time	October or April to May.
Aspect	South or west, sheltered.
Pruning	Shorten excessive shoot growth by half to two thirds in autumn.
Propagation	Ripened hardwood cuttings in shaded cold frame in summer and autumn.
Pests and Diseases	None of note.
Comment	A vigorous scrambling plant noted for its purple, edible, large plum-like fruits produced in warm summers (*see picture above right*). Grows strongly in open conditions in Essex.

Telopea truncata (Tasmanian Waratah)
Hardy evergreen shrub to 4m (13ft).

Flowers	Bright crimson in terminal clusters in June.
Soil	Acid moist.
Planting Time	May.
Aspect	Sunny south or west but not cloistered.
Pruning	Shortening flowered shoots in April.
Propagation	Semi-hardwood cuttings in warm propagator in summer.
Pests and Diseases	Generally free.
Comment	Little grown despite its hardiness. A fine specimen recently recorded at Brockhole in Cumbria.*(see above)*

Teucrium fruticans (Shrubby Germander)
Vigorous hardy evergreen scrambling shrub.

Flowers	Small, bright blue, in terminal racemes throughout the summer.
Soil	Light.
Planting Time	April to May.
Aspect	South or west.
Pruning	Shorten wandering shoots in April and may also be trimmed as shown above.
Propagation	By semi-hardwood cuttings in warm propagator during summer. Similar cuttings in cold frame in autumn.
Pests and Diseases	None of note.
Comment	A particularly pretty combination of the pale blue flowers against the silvery leaves. Proven reliably hardy in East Anglia. Preparations to give cover in exposed gardens would be worthwhile in hard conditions.

Vestia foetida
Slightly tender evergreen bush to 2m (6ft).

Flowers	Primrose, tubular, the thickness of a pencil in April to May.
Soil	Light well drained.
Planting Time	May.
Aspect	South and west.
Pruning	Lightly as required after flowering.
Propagation	By seed or softwood cuttings in warm propagator in early summer.
Pests and Diseases	May come in for the attentions of Red Spider mite.

Comment   A most distinctive early flowering shrub. The small rich green leaves contrasting starkly with the numerous flowers. Needs protection in all but the mostly favourable conditions, though surviving well in East Anglia during recent mild winters. Seedlings abound as the purple seed pods *(see right)* turn brown and discharge their contents.

Wisteria
Hardy, vigorous twining shrubs.

Flowers	Principally May, occasionally late summer.
Soil	Ordinary, enriched with humus material.
Planting Time	Whenever conditions are suitable.
Aspect	South, east or west.
Pruning	Of vigorous growth *(see top picture right)*.
	Should be summer pruned *(see middle picture right) by* tying in shoots required for extension and reducing all others to three buds.
	Follow up with winter pruning in January further reducing the side shoots to two or even one bud *(see bottom picture right)*.
Propagation	Layering in autumn.
Pests and Diseases	Red Spider the most likely in arid conditions
	Birds may damage the fattening buds in mid-winter.

Recommended

floribunda (Japanese Wisteria)	Has fragrant violet-blue racemes.
floribunda 'Alba'	With white flowers on racemes up to 60cm (2ft) long.
macrobotrys	Has scented, lilac racemes often approach 90cm (3ft) in length *(see picture page 98)*
sinensis (Chinese Wisteria)	Has fragrant mauve or lilac racemes.
sinensis 'Alba'	White flowers on moderate racemes.
venusta (see above)	It is extremely vigorous with white slightly scented short stubby racemes. Its individual flowers are the largest of all.

97

Comment   Probably the most popular of all wall shrubs, but unfortunately sometimes reluctant to flower for several years. Grafted plants should always be sought out, they being most likely to perform early. When birds are troublesome stretch black cotton from spur to spur or net.

10
Ornamentals Which Flower During July to September

Abelia
Near hardy bushy evergreen and deciduous shrubs to 1.2m (4ft).

Flowers	Small tubular ranging from white through lilac to orange from July onwards.
Soil	Light well drained.
Planting Time	Late April and May.
Aspect	South-west.
Pruning	As desired in April to maintain an acceptable shape.
Propagation	Layering in spring, softwood cuttings in a warm propagator during summer.
Pests and Diseases	Few if any.

Recommended

chinensis	Low growing with slightly fragrant blush white flowers.
chinensis 'Edward Goucher'	Semi-evergreen with lilac flowers.
x *grandiflora*	Stronger growing with white tinged pink flowers and a measure of fragrance. *(see main picture above)*
x *grandiflora* 'Francis Mason'	A variegated form with the margins of dark green leaves highlighted in gold *(see inset picture above)*.
schumannii	Has lilac-pink, blotched orange flowers and a little scent.

Comment	Valued for their lengthy flowering period and dainty flowers, but liable to damage in a very severe winter, though generally safe.

Albizia julibrissin (Pink Siris or Nemu Tree)
Slightly tender graceful small deciduous tree to 4m (13ft).

Flowers	Fluffy heads of rosy pink.
Soil	Light well drained.
Planting Time	May.
Aspect	South to west.
Pruning	Lightly as required for shapeliness in April.
Propagation	By seed in heat during March and April.
Pests and Diseases	Red Spider may prove troublesome when grown against a warm wall.
Recommended	
'Rosea'	This is considered much hardier than the species.
Comment	A most attractive mimosa-like small tree, flowering on young plants. Fern like foliage adds a distinctive charm when not in bloom. A fine specimen is to be found at the entrance to Cambridge Botanical Gardens.

Aloysia triphylla (Lemon Scented Verbena)
Rather tender deciduous shrub to 3m (10ft).

Flowers	Tiny, purplish, in August.
Soil	Well drained, light.
Planting Time	May.
Aspect	South or west.
Pruning	Hard prune laterals in April, earlier in very favoured areas.
Propagation	Short cuttings with a heel in a warm propagator in spring.
Pests and Diseases	Very vulnerable to Red Spider mite and White Fly.
Comment	Much valued for its strong lemon scent. Of easy cultivation, it is often grown as a biennial.

Ampelopsis
Hardy luxuriant deciduous vine, adhering by clasping tendrils.

Flowers	Insignificant but with light blue berries from September onwards.
Soil	Ordinary.
Planting Time	Whenever conditions are favourable.
Aspect	Any.
Pruning	Shortening strong leaders as required in autumn.
Propagation	Layering in autumn, cuttings of hardwood in cold frame or sheltered border in autumn.
Pests and Diseases	None of note though Red Spider could be troublesome.
Recommended	
brevipedunculata	Has leaves similarly lobed to those of the hop and carries heavy crops of grape-like fruit.
'Elegans'	Attractively variegated, pink and white. Synonymous with 'Tricolour'
Comment	'Elegans' less vigorous, but useful for climbing through an open shrub.

Araujia sericifera (Cruel Plant)
Slightly tender strong growing twining evergreen.

Flowers   Vase shaped, fragrant, creamy white, a little larger than those of Jasmine from
                   July onwards. Followed by large egg-shaped fruits noticeably ribbed which ripen
                   to a yellowish green.

Soil   Ordinary, well drained.
Planting Time   May and June.
Aspect   Clambering through an evergreen shrub facing to south or west.

Pruning   Shortening wayward shoots in April.
Propagation   Softwood cuttings in heated propagator in summer.
Pests and Diseases None known other than night-flying moths in its native Brazil.

Comment   Unusual for its large seed pods filled with silky seed heads. Requiring protection
                   in all but the most sheltered gardens. Surprisingly growing happily in a north-east
                   Essex garden. Given its comon name 'Cruel Plant' due to its entrapment, in Brazil
                   not Essex, of night flying moths which are released in daylight.

Aristolochia macrophylla (Dutchman's Pipe)

A very vigorous hardy twiner climbing to 10m (30ft). Noted for its distinctive heart to kidney shaped foliage

Flowers	Brownish purple, pitcher shaped, in June.
Soil	Ordinary, well drained.
Planting Time	May or September.
Aspect	South, east or west.
Pruning	Customary removal of any dead growths, shortening any excessively long shoots in spring.
Propagation	Division in spring, semi-hardwood cuttings in propagator in July.
Pests and Diseases	No itinerant problems.
Comment	Distinctive and unusual subject with large runner bean-like foliage and unusually shaped flowers. Tailor-made for covering large areas.

Berberidopsis corallina (Coral Plant)

Near hardy evergreen scandent shrub to about 3m (10ft), with leathery heart-shaped leaves.

Flowers	A little larger than a marrowfat pea, deep red racemes from July onwards.
Soil	Neutral to acid.
Planting Time	April to May.
Aspect	Sheltered north-facing.
Pruning	Light shaping as required after flowering.
Propagation	Layering in autumn, softwood cuttings in a warm propagator in April.
Pests and Diseases	None of note.
Comment	A charming climber for training in a shady corner. Requires some protection in severe weather especially from the Midlands northwards.

Billardiera longiflora (Apple Berry)

Slightly tender modest growing evergreen twiner.

Flowers	Yellowish turning to purple from July on *(see above left)*, with blue edible berries in October *(see above right)*.
Soil	Ordinary, well drained.
Planting Time	April to May.
Aspect	South or west.
Pruning	Removal of flowered shoots in April.
Propagation	Semi-hardwood cuttings in warm propagator from April onwards but slow to root.
Pests and Diseases	None of note.
Comment	Well worth a trial in favoured districts. Some protection is required in severe weather especially northwards. Roundish purple fruits in autumn

Callistemon citrinus (Bottle Brush)
Slightly tender bushy evergreen to about 2m (6ft).

Flowers	Deep scarlet in true bottle brush mode, about 15cm (6in) long from June onwards.
Soil	Neutral to acid, enriched and well drained.
Planting Time	April to May.
Aspect	South or west.
Pruning	Removal of flowered shoots as they fade.
Propagation	Semi-hardwood cuttings in warm propagator from May to July.
Pests and Diseases	None in particular, though Red Spider may occur.
Comment	Readily trained against a warm wall away from the easterly wind and it is advisable to give some protection in severe winters. Good examples are to be found in the Midlands and East Anglia.

Campsis
Hardy deciduous climbing or scrambling shrubs to 8m (25ft).

Flowers	Trumpet shaped about 8cm (3in) long, vivid orange and red in August.
Soil	Well drained and enriched with humus material.
Planting Time	May.
Aspect	South, east and west.
Pruning	Hard back to two buds in late winter of all laterals after training main rods.
Propagation	Semi-hardwood cuttings in warm propagator when to hand in spring.
Pests and Diseases	No set problems, usually free.

Recommended

grandiflora	Flowers borne in clusters at the end of the current year's growth. It requires support and tying in.
radicans	*(see above left)* Adheres by aerial roots from new growth. The main rods require fixing from time to time.
radicans 'Flava'	(Yellow Trumpet) A bright yellow version of the above.
x *tagliabuana*	*(see above right)* Has salmon-red flowers on a strong growing plant which requires support.
Comment	Generally regarded as requiring the warmth of the south or west wall though there are several examples of long-lived specimens facing east in East Anglia.

Ceanothus (Californian Lilac)
Hardy bushy deciduous shrub about 3m (10ft).

Flowers	Pink to blue in tight panicles from July to Christmas.
Soil	Ordinary, well drained.
Planting Time	May or September.
Aspect	South, east or west.
Pruning	Reducing previous year's laterals to main rod in April. Leading rods as required.
Propagation	Softwood cuttings in propagator in mid-summer, semi-hardwood cuttings in cold frame in September.
Pests and Diseases	Conspicuous by their absence.
Recommended	
'Gloire de Versailles'	Of modest growth and loosely open habit, carrying pale blue flowers over a long period. *(see lower picture opposite)*
'Henri Desfosse'	As 'Gloire de Versailles' but with rich deep blue flowers. *(see upper picture opposite)*
'Topaz'	Has flowers intermediate in colour with the previous two cultivars.
'Marie Simon'	Carries attractive pinkish orange flowers which are not quite as continuous as the previous ones. *(see above)*
'Perle Rose'	Bright carmine flowers are displayed for several weeks from July onwards.
Comment	In common with the evergreen varieties they are well suited to very dry soils and are a speedy answer for furnishing a wall or fence where there is little frontal room, being hard pruned in spring and flowering on the current year's growth. See elsewhere for earlier evergreen varieties.

Cestrum
Slightly tender deciduous or semi-evergreen modest growing shrubs to 1.5m (5ft).

Flowers	Crimson or yellow from June onwards until frost.
Soil	Ordinary.
Planting Time	May.
Aspect	South or west.
Pruning	Scandent form, main shoots trained to wires and laterals shortened in spring. Upright form, trimming to shape in April.
Propagation	Softwood or semi-hardwood in warm propagator April to July.
Pests and Diseases	Subject to the attentions of both aphids and White Fly.
Recommended	
newellii (see above)	A lax grower of some vigour with a continuous display of crimson tubular flowers, rapidly followed by equally brilliant red berries, both borne at the same time. Ideal for southern and western gardens where it thrives. Protection in winter is advisable.
parqui (see next page)	Produces bright yellow tubular flowers in panicles, especially scented at night. Relatively hardy over all the southern part of the country, survival usually assured if protected at soil level from where it will regenerate after severe frost.
Comment	Very rewarding shrubs well worth the effort, with *parqui* the most reliable. As cuttings root so readily a back-up stock is a wise precaution.

115

Clematis

Hardy deciduous climbers assisted by clasping leaf stems.

Flowers	Ranging from white to pink, blue and red, with varying shades and forms.
Soil	Slightly moist, well drained and rich.
Planting Time	April, May and September.
Aspect	Most will succeed in any position though preferably with some sunshine.
Pruning	Mid-season ones need no more than trimming in March, though if desired may be hard pruned in spring resulting in a few late blooms on a regenerated plant in the first season. Late flowering *viticella* and other varieties may be cut back very hard in March to good effect, or left to luxuriate.
Propagation	Internodal cuttings May to July in warm propagator, layering in autumn.
Pests and Diseases	Aphids are sometimes troublesome on young shoots. Mildew a fairly frequent visitor occasioned by dry soil conditions. Wilt disease sometimes a problem with the large-flowered hybrids.
Recommended	
flammula	Myriads of white starry flowers in August, each the size of a one pence piece. Very vigorous and scented. *(see next page above right)*
jouiniana	A strong growing rambler, but not self supporting. Has abundant crops of pale blue small cup-shaped flowers in clusters from June onwards. *(see above)*
jouiniana 'Cote d'Azur'	Rich azure blue flowers from July onwards.

116

rhederiana	Strong growing, white flowered and pleasantly scented in August *(see lower picture).*
viticella	An indispensable species of rampant climbers. Flowers are white to crimson, somewhat saucer-shaped and 2.5in (6.5cm) across from August onwards.
viticella 'Alba Luxuriens'	White with green tips to tepals. *(see picture above left)*
viticella 'Kermesina'	Rich red. *(see page 119 bottom)*
'Purpureus Plena Elegans'	Lilac-purple, double flowers.
'Rubra'	Crimson

Large Flowered Mid-Season Hybrids

jackmanii	The popular late bloomer with violet purple flowers.
'Julia Coprevnor'	Abundant flowers, purplish black. *(see above right)*
'Mrs Cholmondeley'	Bright blue with a hint of lavender from May onwards. Flowering longer than most with occasional semi-double flowers. *(see above left)*
'Perle d'Azur'	Sky blue smallish flowers with red stamens from June onwards
'Victoria'	Rosy-purple, very free flowering *(see next page top)*.
'Vyvan Pennell'	An outstanding double clematis with violet blue flowers changing to ruby red in the centre. Single blue flowers are often produced at the end of the season.
Comment	The large flowered hybrids form the basis of most collections, such is their spectacular presence. However they are unfortunately liable to wilt disease.

Clerodendron bungeii
Slightly tender deciduous shrub to 2m (6ft).

Flowers	Numerous scented star shaped rose-red florets forming a large boss, 10cm (4in) in diameter.
Soil	Ordinary, well drained.
Planting Time	April to May.
Aspect	Sheltered to south or west.
Pruning	Reduction of flowered stems in spring as growth commences.
Propagation	Removal of short suckers. Semi-hardwood material in warm propagator in summer.
Pests and Diseases	None.
Comment	A most striking end of season shrub enhanced by broad rounded leaves 20cm (8in) in breadth. Not for stylised training but in need of some fence or wall protection. Attractive if allowed to grow through another shrub. Flowers often borne on strong suckers of current season.

Clianthus puniceus (Lobster Claw or Parrot's Bill)

A rather tender strong growing semi-evergreen lax shrub.

Flowers	Bright red, bearing a strong resemblance to a lobster's claw, from July onwards.
Soil	Ordinary.
Planting Time	May.
Aspect	Cloistered south or west-facing.
Pruning	Trimming as required as growth commences in spring.
Propagation	By seed or semi-hardwood cuttings in a warm propagator in summer.
Pests and Diseases	Red Spider a likely trouble.
Recommended	
'Albus'	Creamy white.
'Flamingo'	Deep pink.
'Red Cardinal'	Scarlet.
'White Heron'	White, overlaid green.
Comment	An unusual and dramatic effect when conditions are favourable. Readily trained on cross wires. Needing extra protection in most winters, especially at the base.

Cobaea scandens
A tender perrenial, climbing by tendrils.

Flowers	Purple, bell-like with saucer shaped green calyx from July onwards.
Soil	Ordinary.
Planting Time	May.
Aspect	South or west.
Pruning	Shorten rambling over-wintered shoots.
Propagation	Seed in a warm propagator in March.
Pests and Diseases	Red Spider and White Fly may prove troublesome.
Comment	A useful quick fix for a bare sunny position. While usually grown as an annual, as a perennial it invariably regenerates from the base in late spring. Extremely vigorous.

Colquhounia coccinea
Slightly tender deciduous shrub to 2m (6ft).

Flowers	Tubular, scarlet in late summer.
Soil	Ordinary, light.
Planting Time	September or April.
Aspect	South or west.
Pruning	Removal of dead shoots in March, cutting back to sound buds.
Propagation	By soft to semi-hardwood cuttings in warm propagator in June.
Pests and Diseases	Generally free.
Comment	Liable to damage in severe winters, so protect basal growths. Useful for end of season colour.

Crinodendron hookerianum
A stiffly compact hardy evergreen to about 3m (10ft).

Flowers	Unusually distinct long stalked orange-red ball-like lanterns from June.
Soil	Neutral to acid.
Planting Time	April to May.
Aspect	South or west if well shaded otherwise north.
Pruning	Little more than an occasional trim to maintain shape.
Propagation	Semi-hardwood cuttings in warm propagator May-July.
Pests and Diseases	None of note.
Comment	This is a particularly beautiful and arresting shrub needing wall protection away from the west coast where it thrives from Scotland to Cornwall. Late spring frosts often the cause of disappointment inland.

Decumaria barbara

Hardy semi-evergreen twiner, climbing with aerial roots to around 6m (20ft).

Flowers	White, fragrant fertile corymbs in June and July.
Soil	Rich, slightly moist.
Planting Time	Anytime when favourable.
Aspect	South, west, east and north.
Pruning	Removal of old flower heads and wayward shoots in March.
Propagation	Semi-hardwood cuttings in cold frame in late summer.
Pests and Diseases	Mildew and aphis are rare possibilities.
Comment	Akin to hydrangea though with all flowers fertile, pip-like. Another useful go-anywhere plant.

Dichroa febrifuga
Rather tender deciduous shrub to 1.5m (5ft) overall.

Flowers	Minute, red or blue, on large hydrangea-like heads.
Soil	Ordinary, slightly moist.
Planting Time	May.
Aspect	South, west slightly shaded.
Pruning	Removal of spent flower heads in May, cutting back to first pair of buds only.
Propagation	Semi-hardwood cuttings in summer in warm propagator or shielded cold frame.
Pests and Diseases	None of note, though dormant buds may possibly be affected by botrytis in winter.
Comment	Closely resembling hydrangea macrophylla foliage and growth habit. Flower heads similarly varying according to the acidity or otherwise of the soil between bright red and a rich blue, followed by berries of a similar hue. Unlikely to succeed away from the south-west without much winter protection.

Dregea sinensis
Hardy strong growing deciduous scandent climber.

Flowers	Creamy white, borne in strongly scented clusters in summer.
Soil	Ordinary.
Planting Time	May.
Aspect	South or west.
Pruning	Shorten rampant shoots as required in spring.
Propagation	Short cuttings in warm propagator in mid-summer or by layering.
Pests and Diseases	Generally free.
Comment	A rampant subject suited to most parts of the country given a sheltered wall. Noted for its perfume.

Escallonia

Slightly tender bushy evergreen shrub.

Flowers	Cup-shaped, smallish, variously from pink to crimson and white from June onwards.
Soil	Ordinary.
Planting Time	Whenever favourable conditions apply.
Aspect	South, west or on the coast in the east.
Pruning	Trimming wayward growths in March.
Propagation	Softwood cuttings in warm propagator from May to July.
Pests and Diseases	None apparent.

Recommended

rubens 'Crimson Spire'   Close-growing upright with crimson flowers and leaves which are large for the genus.

rubens 'Donard Star'   Of compact growth with large leaves and rose-pink flowers.

'Apple Blossom'   A particularly attractive and floriferous cultivar recalling the pink and white parts of the fruit in June. Grows to 1.2m(5ft). *(see page 128 lower picture)*

'Donard White'   The pink buds open to pure white florets in June and continue for many weeks. It is a modest sized shrub with small leaves. *(see page 128 upper left)*

'Edenensis'   An improved version of 'Langleyensis' *(see above)*

'Langleyensis'   Gracefully pendent stems with small leaves and flowers of rose-pink.

iveyi   A vigorous large leaved evergreen to 3m (10ft) which produces large panicles of pure white flowers in August, but is rather more tender than most. *(see page 128 upper right)*

Comment   Indispensable for all but the very coldest of gardens inland. Near the coast they are fully hardy. Will regenerate from hard cutting-back. Tolerant of windy sites.

Eupatorium ligustrinum
Slightly tender evergreen shrub to 2m (6ft).

Flowers	Flat heads of small white flowers in late summer.
Soil	Ordinary, lightish.
Planting Time	May.
Aspect	South, west sheltered.
Pruning	Shaping as desired in April.
Propagation	Semi-hardwood cuttings in warm propagator in summer.
Pests and Diseases	None of note.
Comment	A useful addition at summer's end, rapidly growing to a compact bush which makes a light relief to heavy hydrangeas. Hardy in most winters.

Fallopia baldschuanica (Russian Vine)
Exceptionally rampant hardy deciduous twiner.

Flowers	Creamy-white, borne in massed panicles at summer's end.
Soil	Ordinary.
Planting Time	Whenever conditions allow.
Aspect	Any.
Pruning	In March restricting growths as required, snipping off dead heads.
Propagation	Hardwood cuttings in cold frame in early autumn.
Pests and Diseases	Singularly free.
Comment	Particularly vigorous though of some value to cover an eyesore. Will tolerate severe pruning if needed.

Fremontodendron
Rapid growing hardy evergreen shrubs to 4m (13ft).

Flowers	Bowl-shaped, 5cm (2in) in diameter from June to December until frosts intervene.
Soil	Light, well drained.
Planting Time	May.
Aspect	South and West.
Pruning	March, reducing outward growths and shortening leaders.
Propagation	Seed in propagator from March to April. Hard-wood cuttings in cold frame in September.
Pests and Diseases	Little if any though gumming may occur from damaged branchlets.
Recommended	
californica	The common type *(see above right)*.
'Californian Glory'	Bright rich-yellow all summer *(see above left)*.
'Pacific Sunset'	Flowers starting off a deep gold, and gradually fading to rich yellow.
Comment	Very striking though unfortunately notoriously short-lived shrubs, with perhaps a ten years maximum life. The undersides of foliage and young shoots are covered with an irritant indumentum so care should be taken when pruning.

Grevillea rosmarinifolia
Slightly tender evergreen shrub to 2m (7ft).

Flowers	Bright crimson racemes from June onwards.
Soil	Light, neutral to acid.
Planting Time	May.
Aspect	South or west.
Pruning	Trimming as needed in April.
Propagation	Seed outdoors in April, layering in autumn.
Pests and Diseases	Generally free.
Comment	A striking summer-flowering shrub with distinctive needle-like foliage, requiring protection in all but the most favoured gardens.

Hardenbergia violacea (Australian Lilac)
Rather tender, strong growing evergreen twiner with leathery leaves.

Flowers	Violet trusses with white eye akin to those of a Hebe, from late March onwards.
Soil	Ordinary.
Planting Time	May to June.
Aspect	Well sheltered south to west.
Pruning	After flowering, cut away straggly shoots. Sometimes also necessary at summer's end.
Propagation	Semi-hard cuttings in a propagator spring to summer.
Pests and Diseases	None of note.
Comment	Generally regarded as a greenhouse subject although it has endured a fortnight of temperatures well below zero on continuous nights. Well worth a try in favourable areas. Responds to hard cutting-back at any time except winter.

Holboellia

Strong growing hardy evergreen twiner with long lance-shaped digitate leaves.

Flowers	Scented, male pinkish, female white tinged green, bell-shaped on long stalks in July.
Soil	Medium, humus enriched.
Planting Time	April to May.
Aspect	Any.
Pruning	Removal of weak shoots in autumn.
Propagation	Semi-hardwood cuttings in warm propagator in spring.
Pests and Diseases	None of note.
Recommended	
coriacea	Distinctly handsome shrub with edible fruits, which while accepting any aspect is seen to thrive better in full sun.
latifolia	Similar to the above, but less hardy. Hand pollination is recommended for the purple sausage-shaped fruit.
Comment	Produces large purplish plum-like fruit in autumn after a particularly hot summer.

Humulus lupulus (Golden Hop)
A strong growing hardy native twiner.

Flowers	Yellowish-green in clusters in July.
Soil	Rich, well drained.
Planting Time	March.
Aspect	South and west.
Pruning	Cut to base in late April.
Propagation	Seed sown outdoors in April, division of roots in March.
Pests and Diseases	Little if any grown singly, various problems when grown commercially.
Recommended	
'Aureus'	A golden form of the brewers hop.*(see above)*
Comment	An invaluable climber of more or less herbaceous habit. Full sun required to maintain the golden lustre of the foliage. It produces a fair crop of hops when conditions are favourable and self-sown seedlings often appear.

Indigofera
Hardy deciduous scandent shrub.

Flowers	Pea shaped along racemes, rich pink, from May onwards.
Soil	Ordinary, dryish.
Planting Time	Whenever conditions are favourable.
Aspect	South, east or west.
Pruning	Removal of old flower heads in spring, shortening main rods slightly. Will regenerate from the base if damaged by frost.
Propagation	By seed under glass in spring.
Pests and Diseases	None of note.
Recommended	
amblyantha	A fine cascading form *(see back cover lower left)*
dosua	Flowers salmon-pink profusely borne throughout summer. Has attractive pinnate foliage and responds well to wall cultivation. *(see above)*
Comment	An exceptionally pretty and distinctive plant for a sheltered spot, flowering continuously throughout summer on current season's growth.

Itea ilicifolia
Hardy lax evergreen to 3m (10ft).

Flowers	Greenish-white long catkins in late summer.
Soil	Slightly moist, well drained.
Planting Time	April to May.
Aspect	South and west.
Pruning	Removal of spent flower shoots in April.
Propagation	By division or semi-hardwood cuttings in cold frame in autumn.
Pests and Diseases	Seemingly free.
Comment	While the catkins are not particularly arresting, the shrub takes on a distinctly attractive appearance dressed overall in August.

Jasminum officinale (Common White Jasmine)
Strong growing hardy deciduous scandent shrub.

Flowers	White in fragrant clusters from mid-summer on.
Soil	Ordinary.
Planting Time	Whenever conditions allow.
Aspect	South or west.
Pruning	Removing flowered shoots and training in main rods in March or April.
Propagation	Layering in autumn, hardwood cuttings in cold frame in autumn.
Pests and Diseases	Little of note.
Recommended	
officinale affine	An improved form with pink flushed rather larger flowers. *(see above lower)*
'Argenteovariegatum'	Grey-green leaves with white margin.
'Aureum'	Leaves with suffused yellow variegation. *(see above upper left)*
x *stephanse*	A vigorous climber with scented pale pink flowers, followed by shiny black berries. *(see above upper right)*
Comment	Popular late-summer flowerers with the bonus of scent. Tend to get out of hand if not rigorously dealt with after flowering.

Kadsura japonica
A slightly tender twining evergreen shrub to 3m (10ft).

Flowers	Single, cream, in summer with clusters of bright red fruits later.
Soil	Ordinary light.
Planting Time	May.
Aspect	South to west, sheltered.
Pruning	Shortening back over-zealous stems in March.
Propagation	Hardwood cuttings in cold frame in autumn.
Pests and Diseases	Generally free but may be subject to mildew.
Recommended	
'Variegata'	Margins of leaves yellowish-white *(see above)*
Comment	Somewhat similar to *Euonynus fortunei* 'Silver Queen' though with more imposing foliage.

Lapageria rosea

Rather tender modest growing twining evergreen with wiry stems and small and leathery leaves.

Flowers	Outstandingly attractive, trumpet shaped, varying from white to deep pink up to 9cm (3 1/2in) long from late spring to the year's end.
Soil	Peaty, well drained.
Planting Time	May to June.
Aspect	Very well sheltered and slightly shaded to south or west or in a north niche.
Pruning	Shorten wandering shoots in April if necessary.
Propagation	Layering at any time, seed in a heated propagator in spring.
Pests and Diseases	Distinctly free.
Comment	An exceptionally beautiful flower well worth the effort in protected gardens in the south and extreme west. Though free from pests, sooty mould sometimes occurs due to the falling nectar. This is easily, though a little tediously, removed with a sponge.

Lathyrus latifolius (Everlasting Pea)
Hardy herbaceous ornamental pea.

Flowers	White to crimson and violet with appearance of sweet peas, though scentless from June onwards.
Soil	Ordinary.
Planting Time	Whenever conditions are favourable.
Aspect	Any.
Pruning	Remove previous year's growth to ground level in March.
Propagation	Seed sown in spring, division as growth commences.
Pests and Diseases	None evident.
Comment	Very useful scrambling plants for brightening up other shrubs past their flowering stage. Fully herbaceous.

Magnolia grandiflora
Very strong tree-like hardy evergreen shrub.

Flowers	Size of side plates, slightly cupped, creamy white and scented from august onwards.
Soil	Well prepared.
Planting Time	March, April and September.
Aspect	South to West.
Pruning	Careful shaping of wayward branches in March. Overgrown ancient specimens may be severely cut back in March.
Propagation	Layering in autumn, seed in cold frame in spring.
Pests and Diseases	None apparent.
Recommended	
'Exmouth'	A fine form with larger, more strongly scented and earlier flowers than the type. The foliage is large and noticeably glossy.
'Goliath'	Smaller leaves than the above with more vase shaped flowers which bloom in its early stages. *(see above)*
Comment	This is a subject for a very large wall or gable end. In the southern part of the country best planted in the open. Not much in favour with the insurance brigade! Ensure therefore that it is planted no closer than 1m (3ft) and preferably further from the wall as a safety precaution.

Melianthus major (Cape Honey Plant)
Slightly tender evergreen shrub to 2m (6ft).

Flowers	Brownish crimson in terminal spikes in July and August.
Soil	Light rich.
Planting Time	May.
Aspect	South or west, sheltered.
Pruning	Removal of dead stems in spring.
Propagation	Seed in warm propagator in March, cuttings likewise.
Pests and Diseases	Generally free.
Comment	Much valued for its coarse feather-like foliage, making it a strong contribution among other plants. Away from the south west it is often herbaceous though it is prudent to protect the base over winter with straw or similar material.

Mitraria coccinea
Slightly tender evergreen rather bushy procumbent shrub.

Flowers	Brilliant orange red, tube-like, freely borne from June to September.
Soil	Neutral to acid.
Planting Time	May.
Aspect	South or west, sheltered.
Pruning	Occasional pinching-out of wandering shoots.
Propagation	Softwood cuttings in a propagator at most times of the year.
Pests and Diseases	None of note.
Comment	Though a naturally low growing shrub it will climb with the minimum of support. Regarded as slightly tender, it survived unharmed a week of -5 to -7 degrees C (22 to 18 degrees F) in East Anglia.

Mutisia clematis (Climbing Gazania)
Slightly tender evergreen, climbing by leaf tendrils.

Flowers	Bright orange resembling a Gazania in late summer.
Soil	Rich and well drained.
Planting Time	April or October.
Aspect	Favourable niche to south or west.
Pruning	Shortening over-long shoots in April.
Propagation	Semi-hard cuttings in warm propagator from April on.
Pests and Diseases	Subject to slug damage otherwise generally clear.
Recommended	
clematis	A diminutive gazania like flower *(see above)*
ologidon 'Glendoick'	A hardier form with large pink flowers.
Comment	Undoubtedly a most striking shrub which is best grown into an established evergreen. Keep well watered in dry weather.

Myrtus (The Myrtle)
Slightly tender aromatic evergreen shrubs to 4m (14ft).

Flowers	White. fragrant, from July to August.
Soil	Ordinary, well drained.
Planting Time	April to May.
Aspect	South to west.
Pruning	Light trim as required in spring.
Propagation	Cuttings in a warm propagator in July.
Pests and Diseases	Seemingly trouble free.

Recommended

communis (The Common Myrtle) Foliage lustrous green, with flowers followed by purple to black berries.

communis subsp. *tarentina* A much smaller and compact double-flowered form with white berries. *(see above)*

Comment Well worth the effort in the South, needing extra protection from the Midlands northwards. Of easy culture and valued for its long flowering period.

Pandorea jasminoides
Rather tender strong growing evergreen twiner

Flowers	Almost petunia size, funnel-shaped, white suffused lilac in the throat. Flowering thoughout summer in clusters.
Soil	Ordinary, light.
Planting Time	May.
Aspect	South-west.
Pruning	Shortening and training rampant shoots in spring. Will stand hard cutting back.
Propagation	Softwood cuttings or seed in warm propagator in spring.
Pests and Diseases	Often attacked by White Fly.
Recommended var. 'Rosea superba'	A deep pink form reckoned to be hardier than the common variety.
Comment	A most desirable and distinctive climber needing shelter away from the south-west. Strong growing under good conditions.

Passiflora (Passion Flower)
Rampant hardy evergreen climbing by clasping tendrils

Flowers	Spectacular with a religious connotation, blue and white from July onwards.
Soil	Ordinary, well drained.
Planting Time	April to May.
Aspect	South or west.
Pruning	Shorten vigorous trails in April.
Propagation	By suckers, layering or cuttings in a cold frame.
Pests and Diseases	Nothing of note.

Recommended

caerulea	May need some protection from the Midlands northward. Gives heavy crops of orange, egg-shaped but inedible fruits in a favourable season. *(see above flower left, fruit right)*
'Constance Elliott'	A striking all-white form.
edulis 'Purple Granadilla'	Has three-lobed leaves and is notable for its edible purple fruits of smallish plum size.
Comment	The 'Granadilla' only likely to succeed in favourable southern gardens. All will readily regenerate if cut back to ground level. Suckers often produced.

Periploca graeca (Silk Vine)
Strong growing hardy deciduous twiner.

Flowers	Brownish red, though of unpleasant odour, in June.
Soil	Ordinary.
Planting Time	Autumn or March.
Aspect	Any.
Pruning	Removal of weaker shoots in March.
Propagation	Layering in autumn. Ripened cuttings in a cold frame.
Pests and Diseases	Generally free.
Comment	Autumn fruits occurring in pairs with silky tassels. Reputed to have been in cultivation for three centuries. Though deciduous, the leaves last well into the winter, with good colour.

Phaseolus coccineus (Scarlet Runner Bean)

Tender herbaceous twiner.

Flowers	Pea-like, scarlet or white.
Soil	Any, humus rich.
Planting Time	May.
Aspect	Open.
Pruning	Occasionally pinch out the tops.
Propagation	Seed sown under glass in April, outdoors in May or retention of fibrous roots.
Pests and Diseases	Black Fly on occasions and Red Spider if arid.
Comment	A most useful and novel decorative climber most suited to open fencework. On dying back in autumn, roots may be lifted and stored in a frost free greenhouse for replanting in May. Numerous varieties to be found in seed catalogues. Covering the cut-back stems with bark may allow succesful overwintering in mild areas.

Phygelius
Hardy semi-evergreen small shrub.

Flowers	Bearing a resemblance to Penstemon, in late summer.
Soil	Ordinary, well drained.
Planting Time	April and May.
Aspect	South or west.
Pruning	May be lightly trimmed in April or if becoming straggly should be cut to ground level.
Propagation	Soft or semi-hardwood cuttings in warm propagator, division of roots in April.
Pests and Diseases	Aphids sometimes on terminal growths and thrips a frequent pest.
Recommended	
aqualis (Yellow Trumpet)	The stems which are up to 1m (3ft) long, bear loosely pendent yellow flowers on one side of the stem only. *(see inset picture)*
capensis (Cape Figwort)	*(see above)* A more vigorous form with orange red blooms.
'Devil's Tears'	Has deep reddish-pink flowers.
Comment	Easy-going delightfully pretty shrubs flowering until the frosts. Hard cutting to the ground is recommended by Wisley. May need some protection north of the Midlands. The colour range has been extended with the introduction of the Fanfare range of hybrids.

Pileostegia viburnoides
A hardy evergreen, self climbing by aerial roots to 3m (10ft).

Flowers	Creamy white in terminal panicles from August onwards.
Soil	Ordinary.
Planting Time	Whenever suitable conditions prevail.
Aspect	North, south or west.
Pruning	Removal of spent flower heads in April.
Propagation	Semi-hardwood cuttings in propagator from May to July, layering in Autumn.
Pests and Diseases	None of note.
Comment	A telling climber, after a sluggish start, which is at home on a tree trunk as well as a wall, or fence.

Punica granatum (Pomegranate)
Large bushy deciduous shrub to 3m (10ft), rather tender.

Flowers	Orange scarlet in late summer with fruits following occasionally.
Soil	Ordinary, well drained.
Planting Time	May.
Aspect	South or west, well protected.
Pruning	As growth commences in April.
Propagation	Seed in heated propagator in spring, semi-hardwood cuttings in late summer.
Pests and Diseases	Generally free
Recommended	
'Flora Pleno'	A double form. (*see above*)
'Nana'	A much smaller plant to 60cm (2ft).
Comment	Requiring a well protected niche. Unlikely to succeed north of the Cotswolds. Grown more for its striking flowers than the likelihood of fruit, which is seldom produced.

Romneya coulteri (Californian Tree Poppy)
Hardy evergreen semi-shrub.

Flowers	Snow white, saucer-sized with central boss of yellow stamens in July to September.
Soil	Ordinary, well drained.
Planting Time	Whenever conditions are suitable.
Aspect	South, west or east.
Pruning	Removal of spent flower heads and weak shoots in April. May also be cut to ground level at about the same time to invigorate.
Propagation	By division in April, root cuttings in a cold frame in autumn.
Pests and Diseases	Red Spider could be a problem under very dry conditions.
Comment	Often seen as a border plant, it comes into its own when given the shelter of a wall, producing a striking display in late summer.

Salvia
Slightly tender semi-evergreen small shrub to about 2m (6ft).

Flowers	Bright red, smallish, from July onwards.
Soil	Light, well drained.
Planting Time	April to May.
Aspect	South to west.
Pruning	Shaping as desired in April.
Propagation	Softwood cuttings April to July in a warm propagator.
Pests and Diseases	White Fly and Red Spider are likely if set close to a wall.

Recommended

microphylla	The brilliant scarlet flowers demand attention. *(see abovet)*
microphylla var. *neurepia*	Leaves slightly larger, up to 5cm (2in) long and the rather deeper-coloured flowers are similarly larger than the common type.
elegans	Lower growing and much more compact. *(see above right)*

Comment   This is a provider of brilliant colour even though the flowers are not borne in great profusion. The impact is impressive. Best suited to a warm spot where it will survive most southern winters.

Schisandra
Hardy deciduous twining shrubs to 4m (14ft).

Flowers	Pinkish-white or orange-red, borne in May.
Soil	Ordinary, humus enriched, neutral to acid.
Planting Time	September or April and May.
Aspect	South, east or west.
Pruning	Trimming wayward shoots in April.
Propagation	Semi-hard to hardwood cuttings in cold frame in autumn.
Pests and Diseases	None of note.
Recommended	
chinensis	Strong growing with fragrant flowers the size of a 50p coin on long stalks.
rubriflora	Deep crimson, slightly smaller, flowers often followed by scarlet berries.
Comment	Distinctive, each flower with a close resemblance to a miniature Magnolia bloom. Sometimes slow to develop.

Schizophragma hydrangeoides
Strong growing, climbing by aerial roots, deciduous, hardy.

Flowers	Similar to Hydrangea petiolaris but much broader, whitish, in May.
Soil	Ordinary.
Planting Time	September to November, April and May.
Aspect	Any, ideal for a north position.
Pruning	Removal of flower heads in April, reducing other growths as required.
Propagation	Semi-hardwood cuttings in warm propagator in summer.
Pests and Diseases	None of note.

Recommended

hydrangeoides 'Moonlight'	A form with silver marbled foliage.
'Roseum'	A pink-flowered form.
integrifolium	Even more vigorous than the common type.

Comment	Impressive climbers when well established. Usually very slow to develop and needing a degree of extra care.

158

Solanum (Chilean Potato Tree)

Strong growing, slightly tender, deciduous and semi-evergreen shrubs to 4m (14ft).

Flowers	Potato-like, white or blue and yellow, from June to August.
Soil	Ordinary.
Planting Time	April to May.
Aspect	South or west.
Pruning	Reduce leading growths and shorten laterals in April.
Propagation	Softwood cuttings in propagator from mid-summer on.
Pests and Diseases	None of note.

Recommended

crispum 'Glasnevin'	An improved selection with a longer flowering season which starts earlier than the common type.*(see upper left and lower picture)*
jasminoides	A more slender and twining subject, bearing numerous clusters of pale blue flowers.
jasminoides 'Album'	A pure white form of the above which is more frequently grown. *(see upper right)*
Comment	All are rather vigorous but will take severe cutting back. Slightly tender, flowering on current season's growth.

Sollya (Bluebell Creeper)
Evergreen, rather tender, twining shrub to 2m (6ft).

Flowers	Small bell-shaped, azure blue in clusters from June onwards.
Soil	Humus enriched, well drained.
Planting Time	May.
Aspect	South or west, sheltered.
Pruning	Trimming wayward shoots in spring as necessary.
Propagation	Short cuttings in warm propagator mid-summer.
Pests and Diseases	Red Spider and White Fly likely.
Recommended	
parviflora	Has darker blue flowers and narrower leaves.
heterophylla	(Bluebell Creeper) The popular type *(see above left)*.
heterophylla 'Alba'	The white counterpart *(see above right)*.
Comment	By no means fully hardy thus requiring a sheltered niche and best trained on a broad trellis frame. Most suited to the south west, it soon failed in East Anglia, but worthwhile for its striking blue flowers. Planting to grow through an evergreen shrub may prove more successful.

Trachelospermum

Attractive hardy twiners with lustrous evergreen leaves.

Flowers	Jasmine-like, whitish and very fragrant in July and August.
Soil	Light enriched with humus material.
Planting Time	April to May.
Aspect	South or west.
Pruning	Shorten weaker ends of main growths in April.
Propagation	Softwood cuttings in propagator from July to August.
Pests and Diseases	None of note.

Recommended

asiaticum	Strong growing to 2m (6ft) with long glossy leaves.
jasminoides	A less vigorous species with narrower leaves. *(see above left and top right)*
jasminoides 'Variegatum'	Has creamy white blotches and margined leaves. *(see above bottom right)*
'Japonicum'	The most vigorous and largest leaved of the species.
Comment	All requiring a warm aspect to south or west, with likely winter protection north of the Midlands. In the forefront of choice plants but slow to start.

Tropaeolum
Hardy semi-deciduous scrambling perennial.

Flowers	Borne in profusion, scarlet, orange or yellow from June onward.
Soil	Light, neutral to acid, slightly moist.
Planting Time	April and May.
Aspect	Any with a bias to north.
Pruning	Often herbaceous, persistent vines may be trimmed in April.
Propagation	By seed in heat in spring. Division of convolvulus-like roots in autumn, short pieces in small pots in a cold frame.
Pests and Diseases	Slugs at times, otherwise none of note.

Recommended

peregrinum	Bright yellow flowers borne in profusion throughout summer *(see above lower left)*
speciosum (Scottish Flame Flower)	Carries masses of stunning brilliant red nasturtium-like flowers from May to October. It is best in a cool north spot.*(see above upper left)*
tuberosum 'Ken Aslet'	Has slightly larger orange flowers and requires a sunny site. *(see above right)*
Comment	Most rewarding subjects creating a dramatic show when thriving. Often difficult to establish. The rhizomatous roots of *speciosum* tend to wander.

Viburnum
Modest growing hardy evergreen and deciduous shrubs to 2m (6ft).

Flowers	White, very fragrant in rounded flower heads from January onwards.
Soil	Ordinary, slightly moist.
Planting Time	Whenever conditions are favourable.
Aspect	Any, but well suited to a northern one.
Pruning	May be allowed to develop in bush form with minimal attention or trained to wires in autumn.
Propagation	Layering in autumn. Semi-hardwood cuttings July to August in propagator.
Pests and Diseases	Black Fly frequently a problem from overwintering eggs on apical shoots.
Recommended	
x *burkwoodii*	An evergreen, flowering from the early part of the year until May. Readily trained and a useful subject for an open north-facing position.
x *carcephalum*	Deciduous, stiffly branched, and readily trained against an open north-facing position or left to fill a dull corner *(see picture above)*.
Comment	These heavily perfumed early performers are a great joy, doing well in shade. Unfortunately they are mostly grafted shrubs with a particular tendency to sucker. A very close watch is needed; strong shoots from, at, or below soil level are not good news.

Vitex agnus-castus (Chaste Tree)
Slightly tender deciduous shrub to 2m (6ft).

Flowers	Lilac, scented, borne in long tapered spikes from August to September.
Soil	Ordinary, well drained.
Planting Time	September or April.
Aspect	Sheltered to south or west.
Pruning	Shorten flowered shoots in April.
Propagation	Short ripened shoots in autumn in cold frame or greenhouse.
Pests and Diseases	Generally free.
Comment	A striking shrub in late summer resembling a Buddleia. Reckoned to have been grown here for nearly five hundred years. A fine example is on the laboratory wall at Wisley *(see above)*. Makes a telling subject as autumn approaches. Very late to break into growth.

Vitis

Very strong and hardy, climbing by tendrils. Deciduous to 10m (30ft) plus.

Flowers	Insignificant, fruits purplish black grapes.
Soil	Poor for best results, well drained.
Planting Time	Whenever conditions allow.
Aspect	South, west or east.
Pruning	As required to accommodate the vigour immediately after leaf fall. Train in main rods and subsequently cut back laterals to about two buds in November or December.
Propagation	Layering in autumn, hardwood cuttings in cold frame.
Pests and Diseases	Red Spider likely when set against a solid background. Mildew in very hot dry conditions.
Recommended	
vinifera 'Brant'	Has attractive leaf colouration in autumn along with small bunches of sweet grapes.
vinifera 'Purpurea'	Rich bronze-purple foliage. *(see above)*
Comment	Among the most useful of climbers especially for fences.

11
Ornamentals Which Flower During October to December

Celastrus orbiculatus
Hardy deciduous twining shrub to 8m (26ft).

Flowers	Tiny in clusters, greenish-white *(see right)*, with autumnal berries
Soil	Ordinary.
Planting Time	October or March.
Aspect	Any.
Pruning	Shortening and tying wandering shoots as required in March.
Propagation	Layering in spring or autumn.
Pests and Diseases	Generally free.

Comment   A strong grower well suited to a fence. Foliage turns yellow in autumn followed by scarlet and golden fruits which persist for several months over winter, akin to spindle berries *(see above)*.

Clematis cirrhosa *var.* balearica
Modest growing hardy small leaved evergreen.

Flowers	Scented bell-shaped, creamy-white, pendent from October through to May.
Soil	Ordinary with added humus material.
Planting Time	April to May.
Aspect	South or west-facing.
Pruning	Little other than an occasional tidying after main flowering. Overgrown specimens may be hard pruned in May.
Propagation	Seed or internodal cuttings May to early July in warm propagator.
Pests and Diseases	Aphis and Mildew may prove troublesome though generally few problems.
Recommended	
'Freckles'	Heavily spotted orange inside the flowers.
Comment	An outstanding and surprisingly hardy clematis, flowering almost non-stop for many months commencing in autumn. Mulch heavily in winter.

Cotoneaster
Hardy deciduous and evergreen shrubs.

Flowers	White or pinkish with red berries from September onwards.
Soil	Ordinary.
Planting Time	Bare rooted from November to March, pot-grown anytime in favourable conditions.
Aspect	Any.
Pruning	Only as required for training, with occasional removal of excessive breastwood.
Propagation	Seed sown outdoors in spring, cuttings in cold frame in September. By layering in autumn.
Pests and Diseases	Fireblight prevalent in some species.
Recommended	
horizontalis	Deciduous, spreading fish-bone branch form to 2m (6ft). Small flowers, much visited by bees, followed by bright red berries, soon devoured by birds. The foliage assumes bright red in autumn. *(see above)*
horizontalis 'Variegatus'	Similar but with silvery leaves edged cream colouring more dramatically before falling. Berries not quite so freely produced. *(see next page top)*
'Hybridus Pendulus'	Strong growing and evergreen with lax branch work and brilliant red berries which birds favour.

lacteus — A large leaved, strongly growing evergreen bearing clusters of dusky dark red berries in late autumn which are quite bird-proof and remain until April *(see right)*

microphylla — Small leaved evergreen with dark crimson berries, not freely borne, but tending to persist. Its habit is similar to horizontalis.

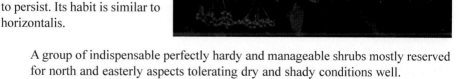

Comment — A group of indispensable perfectly hardy and manageable shrubs mostly reserved for north and easterly aspects tolerating dry and shady conditions well.

Fatshedera lizei

A hardy evergreen of lanky habit to 3m (10ft).

Flowers	White in terminal clusters, late summer.
Soil	Ordinary.
Planting Time	Whenever conditions allow.
Aspect	Any, but well suited to a northerly position.
Pruning	As required, in March, to maintain coverage.
Propagation	Hardwood cuttings in cold frame in autumn and also layering.
Pests and Diseases	Generally free though mildew may occur.
Recommended	
'Variegata'	Leaves with creamy-white margin *(see above)*.
'Annemieke'	Leaves with bold central splash of yellow.
Comment	A useful subject to fill the often bare north position

Hedera (Ivy)
Hardy fast growing evergreen climbers, by aerial roots.

Flowers	Yellowish and inconspicuous, though the black berries are more noticeable.
Soil	Any, well drained.
Planting Time	Whenever conditions allow.
Aspect	Any, though much better variegation occurs in a well lit or sunny position. Most revert to green in deep shade.
Pruning	May be sheared over to bare stems in April if desired, otherwise lightly trim to accommodate in available space.
Propagation	Hardwood cuttings in cold frame or sheltered site in autumn.
Pests and Diseases	Seemingly free. Impatient of water logging.

Recommended

algeriensis 'Gloire de Marengo'	Large rich green leaves bordered creamy-white, often with a fusion of crimson.*(see above left on left of arch)*
colchica	(Persian Ivy)
colchica 'Dentata'	The largest leaved of the genus, muted green.
colchica 'Dentata Variegata'	A striking variant of the above with bluish foliage bordered creamy-yellow *(see next page top)*.
'Sulphur Heart' (Paddy's Pride)	A repeat of the above with a central splash of yellow *(see next page bottom)*.

173

helix 'Glacier'	A small leaved native variant with particularly good adhesive properties. Leaves silvery grey with white irregular margins.
helix 'Goldheart'	A good partner to the above, quickly covering an alloted space. Leaves enhanced by a bold splash of deep yellow, with the young tip growth often clear gold. Clings like a limpet. *(see previous page left, on right of arch)*
'Parsley Crested'	An interesting plain green form with crimped edges.
'Sagittifolia'	Has distinctive three-lobed green leaves which are arrow shaped.
'Sagittifolia Variegata'	Grey green foliage with a creamy margin.
'Tricolour'	Very small grey-green leaves margined white with reddish tones in winter.
hibernica (Irish Ivy)	Vigorous large green leaves.
Comment	Fail-safe subjects for all positions with the due regard for ample light for variegated forms. Assumed damage to brickwork likely only on weak mortar or otherwise of poor condition. Most of the large leaved forms require some additional support, at least in the early years. Those other than native likely to suffer in severe winters but usually regenerate.

Parthenocissus

Strong growing, self-clinging hardy deciduous climbers, for foliage effect.

Flowers	Minute, fruit dark blue, berry-like.
Soil	Ordinary.
Planting Time	When conditions are favourable.
Aspect	Any.
Pruning	Shorten over-zealous growths in November.
Propagation	Hardwood cuttings in cold frame in autumn or outside in a sheltered spot, layering in autumn.
Pests and Diseases	Mildew may prove troublesome in very dry conditions otherwise little of note.
Recommended	
henryana	A striking species with silvery white venation seen to the maximum when planted against a north wall. Often requires some additional support. Provides good autumn colour. *(see inset picture)*
quinquefolia (Virginia Creeper)	Vigorous and giving outstanding autumn colour. Again occasional additional support is needed.
tricuspidata (Boston Ivy)	Strong growing and clinging like a limpet. The most vivid autumn colouring form.
tricuspidata 'Veitchii'	As above though with smaller leaves showing a purple cast on opening. *(see main picture above)*
Comment	Few plants can upstage these for brilliant autumnal hues, unfortunately rather short lived.

Pyracantha (Firethorn)
Strong growing substantial hardy evergreen to 5m (18ft).

Flowers	White in corymbs, hawthorn-like, in May, followed by yellow to red berries.
Soil	Ordinary.
Planting Time	Whenever conditions are favourable.
Aspect	Any.
Pruning	Shortening of excessively long laterals after flowering. May be hard spur-pruned or allowed a degree of bushiness.
Propagation	Seed in cold frame in March, hardwood cuttings in cold frame in autumn.
Pests and Diseases	Often plagued by scab both on berries and leaves and also subject to fireblight and canker.
Recommended	
atlantoides	*(see above left)* A strong upright form with orange-red berries.
'Golden Charmer'	Has bright glossy leaves and early orange yellow berries.
'Orange Glow'	A dense vigorous shrub which produces a heavy crop of berries which persist well through autumn. Resistant to scab.
rogersiana	A heavy cropping form with orange berries.
'Flava'	The yellow-fruited counterpart.
'Soleil d'Or'	*(see above right)* A little less vigorous than most, but with bright golden yellow berries.
'Teton'	Stiffly upright with small yellow-orange berries and leaves. It is disease resistant.
Comment	A most invaluable group of strong and quick growing shrubs. Despite the catalogue of diseases generally remaining free. Mostly self supporting and needing only an occasional fixing.

Senecio scandens

Hardy semi-evergreen scrambling climber.

Flowers	Yellow, like large groundsel flowers, borne in late summer.
Soil	Ordinary.
Planting Time	April and May.
Aspect	South or west.
Pruning	Removal of flowered panicles in April, shaping other growths as required.
Propagation	By softwood cuttings in warm propagator during summer.
Pests and Diseases	None of note.
Comment	A fascinating member of the Groundsel family with the considerable advantage of flowering when most other subjects have come to the end of their season. Will shoot again from the base if cut down by severe weather. Has survived without demur for many years in the Midlands.

Vitis
Hardy deciduous climbers by means of twining tendrils.

Flowers	Tiny, greenish, borne in trusses, and mainly grown for its foliage.
Soil	Ordinary, humus enriched.
Planting Time	Whenever conditions are favourable.
Aspect	South, west or east.
Pruning	Select suitable growths to form main system, shorten ends to firm wood and reduce laterals to two buds in November. Pinch back excessive shoots as desired during the season.
Propagation	Hardwood cuttings in cold frame or sheltered border in November. Layering in autumn, seed under glass in spring.
Pests and Diseases	Mildew and Red Spider occasionally, otherwise these ornamentals are generally problem free.
Recommended	
coignetiae	Rampant twiner with broad rounded leaves that colour dramatically in autumn. It colours best in poorer soils. *(see pictures above)*
Comment	A group of bold climbers quickly filling a barren wall or fence. Trouble free and of easy culture. Leads the field in the autumn colour stakes.

12
FRUIT

The various fruits offer another dimension to furnishing a bare wall or fence, some perhaps in conjunction with ornamentals or more likely as a separate entity in true traditional style.

APPLES

These are best suited to fences rather than walls due to a much greater incidence of Red Spider mite in the warmer, drier environment.

The espalier form *(see above)*, comprising a vertical trunk with lateral arms extending on either side is the usual way of training. These are readily available from leading specialist nurseries and some garden centres. Alternatively one can do one's own thing by planting a maiden, one year old plant, heading it back and gradually forming the lateral limbs. They are suitable for all aspects except north. Allow 4m (13ft) fence space.

Recommended
Dessert
'Discovery'	Very early bright red medium sized fruits, crisp and juicy.
'James Grieve'	Early yellow tinged red juicy fruits. A heavy and regular cropper but poor keeper.
'Red Pippin'	Juicy bright red fruits in mid to late season, similar to Cox's
'Egremont Russet'	Superb flavour, golden green fruits overlaid russet. Mid-season.
'Orleans Reinette'	Late golden yellow flushed red, sweet excellent flavour.
'Sunset'	Late, bright golden yellow aromatic flavour.
'Worcester Pearmain'	Distinctive flavour, bright scarlet fruits early. Best eaten straight from the tree.

Culinary
'Lane's Prince Albert'	Best cooker for training, regular and fine cropper. Good keeper.

Pruning
The principal time to prune is around early August. At this time the leading shoots of the arms are left

alone while all other shoots are cut back to five leaves in anticipation that the remaining leaf buds, or at least one or two, will turn to fruit buds. The shoot is then further shortened to the nearest fruit bud in winter. If none appear either leave alone or cut back to one nearer the arm. The extension shoots being lightly tipped to encourage onward progress in case a fruit bud has formed at that point. Over vigorous specimens may be controlled by either root pruning while dormant or bark ringing in April, *(see page 15)*.

Pollination
With the recommended varieties they should pollinate one another. James Grieve and Worcester Pearmain are particularly good pollinators. Further the ornamental crabs especially Golden Hornet are first rank pollinators and in today's claustrophobic housing estates it would be very strange if there were no pollinators on hand.

Pests and Diseases
Unfortunately apples have much more than their fair share of trials and tribulations. One may wonder after taking note of these whether it is worth the effort. That said the purpose at least in the main for this chapter on fruit is to offer some alternatives to ornamentals for wall and fence furbishment. The odd specimen should not present any insuperable difficulty, though controls are ever becoming more limited. The availability of chemical sprays is in a state of flux. Many of the tried and tested products over the years sadly have or are being withdrawn, therefore growers are advised to seek advice from county horticultural colleges or the Royal Horticultural Society on suitable control measures.

Further, many of the products are stipulated for a specific purpose on a specific crop. To use the material "off the label" is an offence. Judgement on that is in the hand of the potential user.

Pests
Aphids
The Rosy Apple aphid is a frequent visitor at the crucial stage when the leaves and buds are unfurling causing malformed and often useless fruits. *(see right)* One should assume that failing evidence to the contrary they will not have overlooked a chance for a banquet. Control at this stage is paramount.

Apple Sawfly
Almost simultaneously this insidious pest will set up camp in the open flower and deposit its eggs. These hatch within a few days and tunnel into the core area where they banquet until late June when the immature fruitlets and contents fall. Attention at about 80% petal fall is the accredited time for attack.

Capsid Bugs
Nearly always in attendance though instantly dashing for cover when anyone is about, so making their control the more difficult. Their work is characterised by rough russet-like scribblings and patches on fruit and puncturing of foliage.

Codling Moth
This moth or more accurately its larvae enters the semi-mature fruit at the end of June as the sawfly

departs, the female moth having laid its egg thereon a few days before. The grub spends the remaining part of the summer waxing fat on the core area until bringing the supposedly earlier ripe fruit to the ground. Or, perhaps you find the hapless culprit in your first bite. Vulnerable time for the predator is just as it is about to take its first mouthful in late June.

Diseases

Brown rot fungus occasionally puts in an appearance attacking fruit as they ripen and later in store. The only control is to remove and either burn or bury deeply on sight.

Bitter pit is a physiological disorder rather than a disease and due mainly to a shortage of calcium. The condition is typified pin sized brown spots on the fruit with similar spotting in the fruit *(see right)*. Poor drainage may also have a bearing on the disorder.

Canker is manifest by large corky protuberances on limbs and spurs *(see below left)*. Cut away badly affected parts and train in a new shoot. With very heavy infections the tree is best removed.

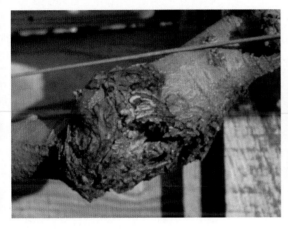

Frost damage causes arresting of the even growth of the fruit giving patchy russeting *(see above right)*

Papery Bark canker is evidenced by the bark exfoliating, peeling outwards, with bad drainage being generally reckoned as a precursor to the malady.

Powdery mildew appears as a white powdery dusting *(see right)* on newly emerging shoots and leaves. Distortion and blackening are symptomatic and left unchecked may cause some defoliation.

Scab appears as chocolate coloured blotches on foliage and later on fruit with a distinct russet feel often developing to severe cracking. Usually it is a greater problem in wet seasons with the rain splashing the spores around *(see right)*.

Woolly aphis or American Blight (Eriosoma lanigerum)
See diseases of ornamentals

APRICOTS

One of the choicest fruits, unfortunately only suited to cultivation in the southern counties. A moderately rich slightly alkaline soil is required and the shoots needing to be trained hard back on either a south or west-facing wall. Usually the latter is preferable. Fully self-fertile though some hand pollinating assistance is recommended. They respond to spur pruning of the main fan ribs in the manner of peaches *(see following page)*.

Recommended
'Moorpark'. The most reliable one for outdoor culture with its juicy fruit ripening late in August. Allow 4m (13ft) wall space at least.

Pests
Little attention is paid by pests other than aphis and these are not usually over troublesome. Spasmodic attacks of caterpillars are always on the cards though not routine.

Diseases
Unquestionably the prime problem here is the sudden die back of limbs often when in the full flush of growth. It is par for the course and such should be cut out at once and a new businesslike looking shoot tied in place.

PEACHES AND NECTARINES

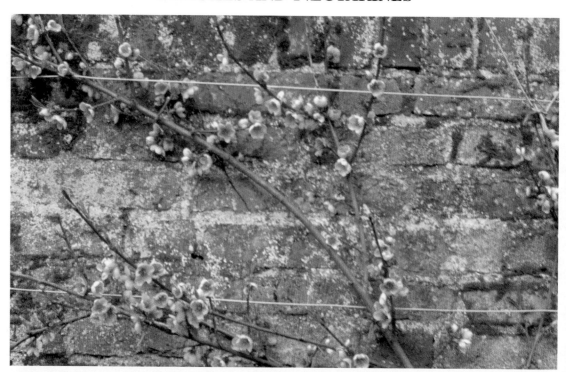

The main difference is that nectarines are rather less hardy than peaches, require the same cosseting as apricots and are usually more successful under glass. They are smoother fleshed, the obvious first impression, and all are self-fertile. All require a very minimum of 4m (13ft) wall space.

Recommended

Peach 'Peregrine'	Given a south or west aspect this is suitable for growing over most of the country. Good juicy flavour mid-August *(see pictures left, flower and fruit))*
Peach 'Rochester'	Heavy crops earlier ripening.
Nectarine. 'Lord Napier'	Richly flavoured, ripening in mid-August.

Pests

Red Spider mite is the most likely in very arid conditions. Frequent clear water spraying to the undersides of the leaves from the beginning of the season is usually a good deterrent.

Diseases

Peach Leaf Curl *(see picture right)* is a notoriously disfiguring disease, attacking as the new foliage opens. Often removing the worst affected leaves at this stage gives sufficient control. Erecting a shelter-like hood at leaf fall with a partial frontal baffle against the rain has a proven track record in its control.

PEARS

Make excellent wall subjects and also on fences some giving a good return north-facing, other aspects suiting well. Two methods of training here are the espalier *(see above)* as for apples and the fan, the latter being much easier to develop on a DIY basis. Allow 4m (13ft) wall or fence space.

Recommended

'Beurre Hardy'	Large conical greenish-yellow flushed red fruit of good flavour. Strong grower and heavy cropper.
'Concorde'	New variety similar to 'Conference' and a heavy cropper, juicy. Mid-season.
'Conference'	Established favourite green lightly russeted fruit. Pine flavour. Mid-season.
'Doyenne du Comice'	Large juicy fruit exceptional flavour. Late season. *(see back cover, lower right)*
'William's Bon Chretien'	Yellow fruits ripen early with the familiar musky flavour of the 'Bartlett Pear' of the canning industry to which it owes allegiance.
'Winter Nellis'	Small green, changing to yellow, of excellent flavour. Very late. Will give a good performance on a north-facing fence or wall.

Pollination

'Conference' is self-fertile, a good pollinator, and will set a good crop alone. Others will pollinate one another and further enhance this variety..

Pruning

Main pruning takes place in late summer when all the current season's shoots, excepting those needed for extension, are reduced to just above three leaves from the basal cluster. These shoots are then cut back hopefully to a formed fruit bud in winter. Any resurgent growths removed and extension ones cut back by a third.

Pests

Pear Midge. A near microscopic insect that lays its eggs into the opening flower. Subsequently becoming established in the core region and eventually bringing the fruit to the ground prematurely. The midge maggots remain in the soil for up to two years during which time regular hoeing may well introduce them to a foraging bird, otherwise spray into the flower when most of the petals have fallen.

Pear slugworm. A miserable slug-like caterpillar that skeletonises the leaves. A watchful eye and a little handpicking may suffice.

Sundry other marauding **caterpillars** and **capsid bugs** may from time to time put in an appearance.

Birds. The downside of encouraging tits into the garden is their obsession with this fruit. A simple shield of cardboard affixed on top of each fruit often suffices. Enclosing one or more fruits in a fine meshed netlon bag works one hundred percent. Overall netting needs to be firmly tied lest any slight opening acts as a gateway and often enmeshing the bird.

Wasps. These are only likely to attack over ripe fruit which should have been picked anyway.

Diseases

Pear Scab. A very common and debilitating disease evident by smallish dark brown patches on both leaves and fruits. Some chemical control or preferably preventative should be applied early in the blossom stage and again ten days of so later.

Pear Canker. Rough cankerous growths often the result of embedded scab disease to which it is linked. Badly affected limbs should be removed as further die back will follow spreading the infection.
Badly drained soils are often the precursor to the trouble. Despite the above I have found the pear to be one of the easiest most trouble free fruits to grow.

Brown Rot. Remove any fruit so affected and bury deeply.

Pear Rust. A lttle known disease *(see picture right)* which has surfaced in recent years. The first evidence is of orange, five pence-sized, spots on the surface. Later, horn-like growths appear underneath producing spores. These infect the evergreen *Juniperus sabina*, overwinter and reinfect the following year. Mild attacks may best be dealt with by removing infected foliage if minimal. In severe cases, cankerous growths appear on the branches.

BRAMBLE FRUITS

These lend themselves to easy training and general management though demanding of considerable space. Blackberries *(see a variegated one above)*, Loganberries and Tayberries are best trained on the three wire horizontal system, these being deployed at 60cm, 95cm and 120cm (2ft, 3.5ft and 5ft). The canes are then trained on the two top wires by the rope system, either twisting them around the wires or securing by occasional ties. The lower wire is used to train the current season's growths which supplant the old fruited ones immediately following cropping. An exception is with the blackberry which fruits on canes one or more years old. One wire may therefore be reserved for one year old and the other for those of two years.

Loganberries and Tayberries crop only on one year old canes. This offers another system of training, that of the fan leaving the open central vee shape in which to tie in the newly developing shoots which after cropping are opened out to the fan structure, previously arranged. A minimum of 5m (16ft) should be allowed. A well worked fairly rich soil is required for these fruits.

Pests

Principal of these is the Raspberry Beetle which lays its eggs in the open flowers. Control is at the 80% petal fall stage. Leaf miner *(see right on Tayberry)* can cause havoc; infected leaves are best removed on first sight. Other itinerant caterpillars may put in an appearance though not on a regular basis. Fort Knox protection against birds is vital at fruiting stage.

Diseases

These are relatively few with Cane Spot being the principal worry. This is first evident as purple spotting on the canes and subsequent spreading onto the newly developing canes.

Recommended

Blackberry

'Loch Ness'   A recent introduction of stiffish growth and so suited to fan training which crops heavily from late August.

'Oregon Thornless'   A lighter cropper of sharp flavour. Vigour is modest while the leaves are attractively akin to parsley.

Loganberry

'Loganberry LY 59'   Deep red fruit from July recommended for preserving.

'Loganberry Thornless' Similar to the above though minus the hassle of prickles.

Tayberry

Much heavier cropping, loganberry type fruit. Large, nearly black and slightly less sharp *(see below left)*.

Wineberry

Raspberry-like fruit borne in tight terminal clusters on strong canes to 1.25m (5ft). Best grown against a warm wall to south or west. *(see below right)*.

CHERRIES

These may follow the same pattern as for plums. Sweet varieties being best on a south or west wall, while the sour or culinary ones will take any aspect, these being less vigorous than the former. Pests and diseases are usually only a minor irritant. Allow 6m (20ft) minimum.

Recommended
'Summer Sun'   A new, sweet variety with dark red fruits that hang well, early July.
'Stella'   A slightly later variety with similar coloured fruits, good dessert.
'Morello'   The established culinary, or sour, variety and the one-time basis for Cherry Brandy.
                     A standby for a north-facing wall.

Pollination
'Summer Sun' and 'Stella' are the only two self-fertile sweet cherries and either will crop well in isolation. Equally 'Morello' is self-fertile and most favoured for culinary use. Other sour cherries are self-fertile.

Pruning
Mainly as for plums though they also form spurs which may be pruned back to a fruit bud after picking. Root pruning should be regarded as routine to control their vigour, particularly of sweet varieties. This is carried out after leaf fall and in the earlier years may take the form of actually prising out the root ball, severing strong roots and dropping back, then treading firm.

Pests
Cherry Blackfly is often a nuisance early in the season. From time to time some of the plum predators may attack.

Diseases
Bacterial Canker and Silver Leaf are the principal ones. Treat as for plums.

CURRANTS

Both red and white currants lend themselves to wall or fence training. The usual form being either cordon or double U pattern. Any aspect being suitable with the advantage that those on a northerly position will hold the fruit much longer. Suited to almost any soils given good drainage.

Recommended
Redcurrants.
'Laxton's No 1'   Standard variety giving heavy yields beginning of July. Resistant to mildew.
'Rovado'   A recent introduction showing disease resistance which crops heavily at the beginning of August.

Whitecurrants.
'White Versailles'   Large light-yellow fruit, early July.

Pollination
These currants are all self-fertile so no problems.

Pruning
Lateral shoots should be pruned back to about 10cm (4in) at the end of June and further shortened to one or two buds in November. Leading shoots being shortened by about one third, keeping an open vase-shaped bush on a leg.

Pests
Aphids are fairly regular visitors early in the season
Currant Clearwing Moth and the Currant Shoot Borer arrive from time to time causing branchlets to wilt.

Diseases
Rust is a fair possibility. The ubiquitous Coral Spot may well put in an appearance living on dead as well as living material. Its presence being aptly described by its name.

FIGS

Strong growers requiring a warm wall from the Midlands southwards. Almost the sole form is that of a fan trained specimen to which they lend themselves readily. Fruit is borne on growths made the previous season. Training therefore hinges on cutting out much of the old fruited wood and tying in strong new ones which is done soon after leaf fall. A modicum of older rods may be retained making use of their newer side shoots displaying the embryo figs that will form next year's crop. It is worth bearing in mind that most fruitlets remaining after leaf fall will duly drop off by the year's end except those about the size of a pea which will become next year's crop. Very vigorous plants may require root pruning as described for cherries.

Recommended
Brown Turkey *(see above)*

Pests and Diseases
Happily there is very little to report here. Blackbirds have a discerning palate for the fruit and some protection may be needed against their forays. A minor problem is that figs do not ripen as a crop, tending to come in small numbers. Mildew can occasionally be found on terminal shoots under stagnant conditions late in the dormant period.

GOOSEBERRIES

Make excellent wall and fence subjects lending themselves to restrictive training in much the same manner as red and white currants. They may also be cordon grown *(see picture above)* and are suited to most soils apart from those likely to become waterlogged. Perhaps more than most fruits they have a particular requirement for ample potash. Any aspect is suitable with the advantage of later fruits from one facing north.

Pollination
All are self-fertile so no problems.

Pruning
Precisely as for redcurrants, though leaving the laterals slightly longer in the formative years.

Pests
Birds can prove a near disaster attacking the fattening buds from November onwards. For this reason

pruning is often recommended to be deferred until March. Bullfinches and Sparrows are the main offenders with Blackbirds, the great fruit connoisseurs taking their toll when ripe.

Gooseberry Sawfly
The arrival of this obnoxious creature is indicated by an overnight removal of almost all the foliage from the centre outwards. The caterpillars hatch from eggs laid on the foliage at blossom time.

Magpie Moth
Caterpillars of this dainty ethereal moth are sometimes in attendance though not quite so voracious as the sawfly. Other vagrant moth larvae occur from time to time including the Winter Moth.

Aphids
Always on the look out for a free breakfast they commence activities on the softer young leaves, causing distortion and if severe will cripple the extension growth.

Diseases
American Gooseberry mildew
A serious and frequent attacker first noticed on the newly formed foliage and later the berries. This is seen as brown patches and needs attention in the earliest stage. As it tends to over-winter on the apical tips, the standard pruning for trained bushes will for the most part remove any infection.

Die Back
Not a serious problem though it may appear from time to time arriving from other infected material nearby.

Recommended

'Careless'	A heavy cropping variety of good flavour and general use which is ready towards the end of July for dessert purposes.
'Invicta'	A recent introduction laying claim to disease resistance which produces vigorous heavy crops in late July.
'Leveller'	Considered to have the best flavour, but a rather weak grower, which produces fruits, a pleasing yellow green, in late season
'Whinham's Industry'	A particularly heavy cropper, with berries rounded and dusky red, for general usage especially culinary.

GRAPES

These succeed from the Midlands southwards given a warm well drained site. They are of rapid growth, self-fertile and readily trained. Two methods are espalier or cordons (single or double U shaped). The espalier, while taking longer to develop, is more suited to fit under a window or where a lengthy space is to hand. Cordons are formed by allowing a vertical shoot to develop side shoots at 45cm (18in) intervals over several years, the main stem being shortened in November to force new growths.

All major pruning should be carried out at that period whatever the method. Subsequent stopping to curtail the side growths is done when the flower trusses are observed in spring, pinching out the centre two leaves past the truss. Further side shoots are pinched at one leaf. If no truss is formed stop back at six leaves.

Recommended

'Black Hamburg'   Dusky crimson, sweet and juicy, berries are freely borne in early September. It is best on a warm sheltered wall. *(see above)*

'Royal Muscadine'   An easy doer which produces smallish sweet green grapes.

Pests

Red Spider is a prevalent foe under arid conditions but frequent misting under the foliage will help deter its arrival.

Diseases

The curse is powdery mildew often brought on by over cloistered conditions and dryness at the root.

KIWI FRUIT
(Chinese Gooseberry)

A distinct newcomer to the established range of fruits and a vigorous twiner, it is a worthwhile consideration for a sheltered position. A fine very heavy cropping specimen is to be seen in Stourton Garden, Wiltshire, grown as a standard in a relatively open site. Soil of average fertility and good drainage is required while pollination is rather confused, some plants are male, some female and some polygamous. These latter ones bear fruit of poorer quality than the accredited female forms, which need a nearby male. Best trained in close proximity on horizontal wires.

Good examples of well-trained specimens may be seen at Wisley.

Recommended
'Hayward' and 'Tomuri' are female and male varieties respectively. They should be planted together in close proximity.

Pests and Diseases
Seemingly pest and disease free.

PLUMS

Much too vigorous for fence work and best suited to a warm wall, facing to south or west. Their vigour will need to be controlled by regular root pruning. The fan shape is standard as for peaches *(see page 186)*. Allow a minimum of 6m (20ft) wall space.

Recommended

'Czar'	Has smallish purple fruits ripening in August which are fair eating and particularly good for culinary usage. It is self-fertile and seldom fails to crop.
'Dennistons Superb'	Has medium sized fruits, greenish-yellow, with a slight greengage flavour. It is self-fertile and ready mid-August.
'Marjorie's Seedling'	The large purplish fruits are of excellent flavour in late September and into October. It is self-fertile.
'Victoria'	The doyen of the tribe and when well grown has fruit of unsurpassed quality. Unfortunately it is very subject to silver leaf disease which affects trees at almost any age. Self-fertile, though not the most reliable cropper, and ready late August.

Pollination

As all those described are self-fertile and few problems arise given absence of cold drying winds or frost at blossom time, setting a good crop on their own, while often better with a partner.

Pruning

Initially spread the branch-work out like the ribs of a fan. Subsequently rub out newly emerging buds on the wall side and to the front as growth commences. Developing side shoots need pinching at about six leaves and later shortening after cropping, tying in other laterals needed to extend the system. Tip leading shoots and root prune when dormant.

Pests

Aphids must have the claim for the biggest nuisance demanding a close inspection from early in the season.

Caterpillars A watchful eye will also be required for the attentions of various leaf eating caterpillars, notably those of the Winter Moth, Lackey Moth and Vapourer Moth, though not serious pests. Grease bands applied in August give a fair measure of control.

Red Plum Maggot

A low incidence though nauseating caterpillar, it feeds on the fruit just under the skin and may be found towards picking time.

Plum Sawfly

Another real pest attacking the embryo fruitlets in the blossom stage, but fortunately not very common. Control as for apples, by spraying into open flowers.

Red Spider

This is the bane of all gardeners especially when plants are grown in rather arid conditions such as on a warm wall. Attack is typified by an ashen look of the foliage particularly on young leaves. Severe attacks will show up the minutely fine webbing spun from leaf to leaf and little effective control is available. Regular misting of leaf undersides should prevent a serious build-up.

Diseases

Bacterial canker
An occasional visitor arising through badly made prunings and bark damage, though seldom a real problem.

Brown rot
A fairly common problem with plums, simply remove on sight and bury.

Gumming
A physiological disorder often encountered in some seasons, the gum arising from the stones and sometimes from the tree branches.

Shot Hole fungus
A frequently occuring disease where holes slightly larger than a pin-head appear in mid-summer. Usually ascribed to high humidity.

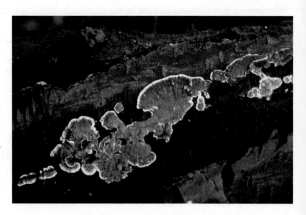

Silver leaf
Aptly describes the problem with the silvering brought on by the development of an air space under the leaf surface. The most susceptible is 'Victoria' and no control is available. Removal of infected branches *(see right)* until the tell tale internal brown staining is by-passed sometimes helps. Usually the end is nigh.

Award of Garden Merit (AGM)

A large proportion of the plants described are repecients of the AGM. This is a prestigeous accolade, bestowed by the Royal Horticultural Society (RHS) on plants regarded as superior forms for general cultivation. For the convenience of the connoiseur the following climbing plants are current recipients.

Abelia x *grandiflora*
Abelia x *grandiflora* 'Francis Mason'
Abutilon vitifolium 'Tennants White'
Abutilon 'Kentish Belle'
Abutilon megapotamicum
Albizia julibrissin 'Rosea'
Actinidia kolomitka
Camellia japonica 'Alba Simplex'
Camellia japonica 'Jupitor'
Camellia japonica x *williamsii* 'Donation'
Camellia japonica x *williamsii* 'St. Ewe'
Campsis radicans 'Flava'
Campsis x *tagluabuana* 'Madame Galen'
Carpenteria californica
Ceanothus 'Delight'
Ceanothus x *delileanus* 'Gloire de Versailles'
Ceanothus x *delileanus* 'Topaz'
Celastrus orbiculatus
Cestrum parqui
Chaenomeles x *superba* 'Pink Lady'
Choisya ternata
Choisya ternata 'Aztec Pearl'
Choisya ternata 'Sundance'
Cladrastis lutea
Clematis armandii 'Snowdrift'
Clematis alpina 'Francis Rivis'
Clematis 'Barbara Jackman'
Clematis cirrhosa var. *balearica*
Clematis cirrhosa 'Freckles'
Clematis 'Comtesse de Bouchard'
Clematis flammula
Clematis 'Henryi'
Clematis x *jouiniana* 'Praecox'
Clematis macropetala
Clematis macropetala 'Markhamii'
Clematis 'Mme Julia Correvon'
Clematis montana 'Elizabeth'
Clematis montana grandiflora
Clematis montana var. *rubens*
Clematis 'Mrs Cholmondeley'
Clematis 'Nelly Moser'
Clematis 'Niobe'
Clematis 'Polish Sprit'
Clematis rehderiana
Clematis tangutica
Clematis 'Ville de Lyon'
Clematis viticella 'Alba Luxurians'
Clematis viticella 'Kermesina'
Clerodendron bungei
Cotoneaster horizontalis
Cotoneaster horizontalis variegata
Cotoneaster lacteus

Crinodendron hookerianum
Cytisus battandieri
Daphne bholua
Desfontania spinosa
Eriobotrya japonica
Escallonia 'Apple Blossom'
Escallonia iveyi
Euonymus fortunei 'Emerald Gaiety'
Euonymus fortunei 'Emerald n Gold'
Euonymus fortunei 'Silver Queen'
Fatshedera x *lizei* 'Variegata'
Forsythia x *intermedia* 'Suspensa'
Fremontodendron 'California Glory'
Garrya eliptica 'James Roof'
Hebe hulkeana
Hedera colchica 'Dentata Variegata'
Hydrangea petiolaris
Jasminum nudiflorum
Jasminum officinale
Jasminum stephanense
Kerria japonica 'Pleniflora'
Indigofera amblyantha
Indigofera heteranth
Leptospernum scoparium
Lonicera japonica 'Halliana'
Lonicera periclymenum 'Belgica'
Lonicera periclymenum 'Serotina'
Lonicera x *tellmaniana*
Melianthus major
Olearia macrodonta
Osmanthus x 'Burkwoodii'
Paeonia lutea var. *ludlowii*
Parthenocissus tricuspidata
Parthenocissus henryana
Passiflora coerulea
Phlomis fruticosa
Phygelius capensis
Pieris 'Forest Flame'
Pileostegia viburniodes
Punica granatum 'Floro Pleno'
Ribes speciosum
Rosmarinus officinalis 'Miss Jessop's Upright'
Solanum crispum 'Glasnevin'
Solanum jasminoides 'Album'
Trachelospermum jasminoides
Viburnum carcephalum
Vitis 'Brandt'
Vitis coignetiae
Vitis vinifera 'Purpurea'
Wisteria florabunda 'Macrobotrys'
Wisteria sinensis

Glossary

Apical   The tip of a leading shoot.

Bass   Tying material produced from pine trees as raffia.

Breastwood   Shoots pointing forward from wall or fence.

Corymb   The flat topped cluster of a flower.

Fillis   Garden string.

Indumentum   The velvet-like dusting on the leaf underside.

Panicle   A wedge shaped flower cluster.

Ph factor   Relates to the hydrogen ions in the soil indicating its acidity or alkalinity. The logarithmic scale operates from 1 to 14 with 7 as neutral and 14 as extreme alkalinity.

Procumbent   Laid upon the ground.

Rod   A cane-like stem.

Scandent   Long loose growths deployed fan-like.

Terram   A geo-textile blanket-like material.

Venation   The arrangement of the leaf veins.

Index

Common names